BLOCKCHAIN ECOSYSTEM

BLOCKCHAIN ECOSYSTEM

M. Madhumathi | U.A. Ranjni

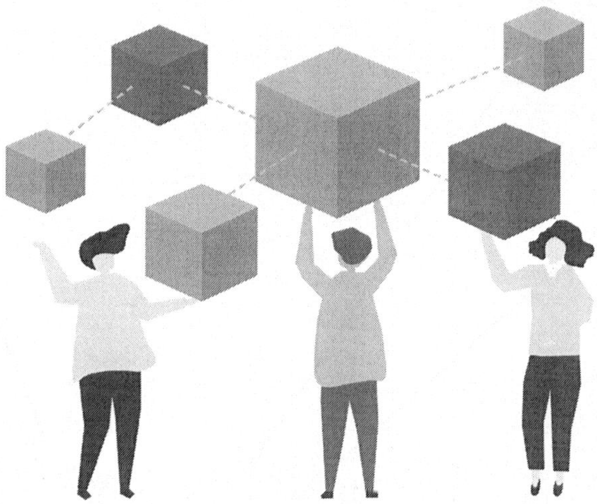

KHANNA BOOK PUBLISHING CO. (P) Ltd.
4C/4344, Ansari Road, Darya Ganj,
New Delhi, India

Sathyabama Institute of Science and Technology
Jeppiaar Nagar, Rajiv Gandhi Salai,
Chennai, Tamilnadu, India

Dear Readers,

To prevent the piracy, this book is secured with HIGH SECURITY HOLOGRAM on the front title cover. In case you don't find the hologram on the front cover title, please write us to at contact@khannabooks.com or whatsapp us at +91-99109 09320 and avail special gift voucher for yourself.

Specimen of Hologram on front Cover title:

Moreover, there is a SPECIAL DISCOUNT COUPON for you with EVERY HOLOGRAM.

How to avail this SPECIAL DISCOUNT:

Step 1: Scratch the hologram
Step 2: Under the scratch area, your "coupon code" is available
Step 3: Logon to www.khannabooks.com
Step 4: Use your "coupon code" in the shopping cart and get your copy at a special discount
Step 5: Enjoy your reading!

Thanks,
Khanna Publishing House

ISBN: 978-93-55384-11-9

Blockchain Ecosystem
by **M. Madhumathi; U.A. Ranjni**

First Edition: 2025

To view complete list of books, please scan the QR Code:

Published by:
Khanna Book Publishing Co. (P) Ltd.
CIN: U22110DL1998PTC095547

Visit us at: www.khannabooks.com
Write us at: contact@khannabooks.com

Printed in Bharat.

Preface

In recent years, the world has witnessed a remarkable transformation in the way we think about digital assets, transactions, and decentralized networks. At the heart of this revolution lies blockchain technology – a foundational innovation that has reshaped industries, from finance to supply chains, healthcare to governance, and beyond. Blockchain offers more than just the promise of secure, transparent, and immutable record-keeping; it introduces a new paradigm for trust, value exchange, and collaboration without relying on central authorities or intermediaries.

This ecosystem, fueled by blockchain technology, has blossomed into a vast, interconnected network of developers, businesses, entrepreneurs, and enthusiasts, each contributing to a shared vision of decentralization and democratization of data. Through its core principles—decentralization, transparency, and immutability—the blockchain ecosystem is laying the groundwork for a more inclusive digital future where individuals have greater control over their assets, identity, and interactions.

This book aims to explore the intricate and interconnected nature of the blockchain ecosystem, shedding light on its complexities, opportunities, and future directions. Whether you are an enthusiast, entrepreneur, developer, or policymaker, understanding the blockchain ecosystem is essential for staying ahead of the curve in an increasingly decentralized world.

Contents

Network and Security

UNIT 1

1.1 ADVANTAGES OVER CONVENTIONAL DISTRIBUTED DATABASES

Conventional distributed databases replicate data across multiple nodes but still rely on a central authority for administration, and they often lack built-in immutability. In contrast, blockchain technology offers:

- **Decentralization:** Every participant (node) holds an identical copy of the ledger. No single entity has control, eliminating central points of failure.
- **Immutability:** Transactions are cryptographically sealed in blocks. Changing one block would require recalculating all subsequent blocks and obtaining consensus from the majority of nodes.
- **Transparency & Auditability:** All transactions are recorded in a chronological, publicly verifiable ledger (for public blockchains). This enhances trust and simplifies auditing processes.
- **Security:** Data is secured using cryptographic hash functions and digital signatures. Even if an attacker compromises one node, the distributed nature of the network ensures the ledger's integrity.
- **Reduced Intermediaries:** By eliminating central intermediaries (banks, administrators), transactions can be processed directly between peers, potentially lowering costs and improving efficiency.
- **Data Replication:** In distributed databases, replication is usually managed by a central coordinator. In blockchain, replication is done peer-to-peer, ensuring every node independently verifies transactions.
- **Cryptography:** Cryptographic hash functions (e.g., SHA-256) bind blocks together, making tampering computationally prohibitive.
- **Consensus Requirements:** Instead of trusting a central administrator, blockchain systems require consensus across nodes (discussed in detail later)
- **Resilience to Single Points of Failure:** Since no one node controls the system, the failure or compromise of a single node does not disrupt the overall network.
- **Enhanced Trust:** In a trustless environment, participants do not need to rely on a central authority to validate transactions. Instead, the cryptographic underpinnings and consensus algorithms ensure that all records are accurate and tamper-proof.

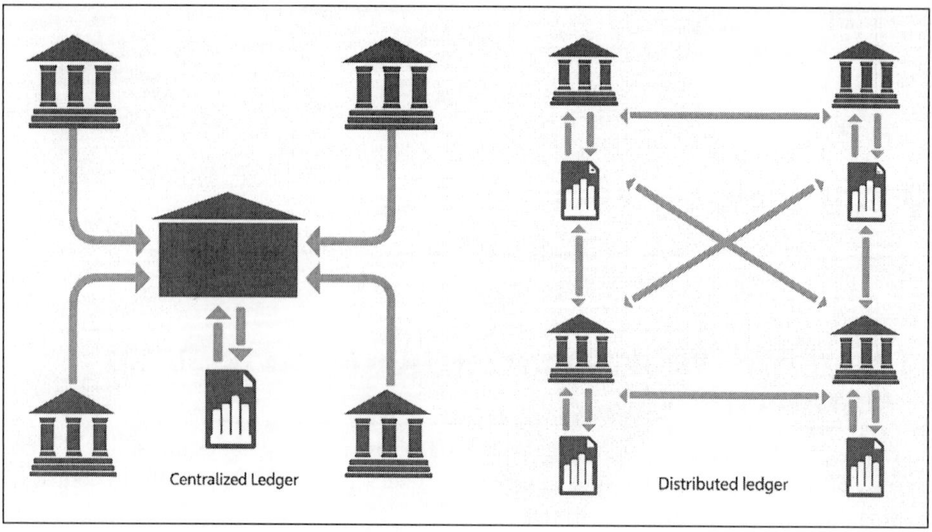

Fig. 1.1: Conventional Distributed Database vs. Blockchain

1.2 BLOCKCHAIN NETWORK ARCHITECTURE

Core Components

- **Nodes:** The backbone of the network. Each node runs blockchain software, maintains a copy of the ledger, and participates in consensus. Nodes can be full nodes (store complete chain) or lightweight nodes (store partial data).
- **Blocks:** Units of data containing a group of transactions. Each block has two main parts:
  - **Header:** Contains metadata (version, previous block hash, Merkle root, timestamp, difficulty bits, nonce).
  - **Body:** Contains the list of transactions.
- **Cryptographic Hashing:** Each block's header is hashed. The hash of the previous block is stored in the current block's header, forming a chain. A minor change in a block's data changes its hash dramatically, ensuring immutability.
- **Smart Contracts (if applicable):** Self-executing contracts stored on the blockchain that run when predefined conditions are met. These extend blockchain functionality beyond simple transactions.
- **Consensus Mechanism:** Protocols (e.g., PoW, PoS) that ensure all nodes agree on the ledger's state without a central authority.
- **Merkle Trees:** A data structure used to efficiently summarize and verify the integrity of large sets of transactions. The Merkle root is stored in the block header.
- **Network Communication:** Nodes communicate over a peer-to-peer (P2P) network using protocols that propagate new transactions and blocks across the network rapidly.

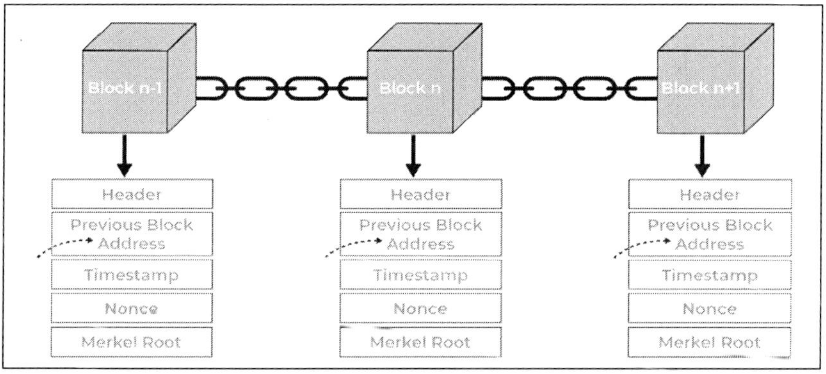

Fig. 1.2: Blockchain Network Structure

1.3 MINING MECHANISM

Mining is the process by which transactions are validated, bundled into blocks, and permanently added to the blockchain ledger. In Proof-of-Work (PoW) systems—the most widely known mining model used by Bitcoin—miners compete to solve complex cryptographic puzzles. The first miner to solve the puzzle earns the right to add the new block to the chain and is rewarded with newly minted cryptocurrency along with transaction fees.

Mining Process

- **Transaction Collection:** Nodes collect unconfirmed transactions from the network.
- **Block Formation:** These transactions are grouped into a candidate block.
- **Proof-of-Work (PoW):** The most common mechanism (used in Bitcoin). Miners solve a cryptographic puzzle by varying a nonce until the hash of the block header meets a predefined difficulty target.
    - **Difficulty Adjustment:** The network periodically adjusts the difficulty so that blocks are mined at a steady rate (e.g., Bitcoin targets one block every 10 minutes).
- **Block Propagation:** Once a miner finds a valid nonce, the block is broadcast to other nodes, which verify its validity.
- **Reward Distribution:** The successful miner receives a block reward (new cryptocurrency coins) and transaction fees.

Alternative Mining Mechanisms

- **Proof-of-Stake (PoS):** Validators are chosen to create a block based on the amount of cryptocurrency they hold (their stake). This reduces energy consumption compared to PoW.
- **Delegated Proof-of-Stake (DPoS):** Stakeholders vote for delegates who validate transactions and create blocks.
- **Practical Byzantine Fault Tolerance (PBFT):** Used in permissioned networks, where a fixed set of validators agree on the next block through a series of voting rounds.

- **Hybrid Models:** Some networks combine PoW and PoS, or incorporate sharding and DAG (Directed Acyclic Graph) techniques to improve scalability and security.

Technical Details

- **Hash Functions:** Mining relies on hash functions (like SHA-256) which produce a fixed-length string from input data. They are deterministic, collision-resistant, and sensitive to input changes.
- **Energy Consumption:** PoW mining is resource-intensive, leading to concerns about energy usage. PoS is seen as a more sustainable alternative.

1.4 DISTRIBUTED CONSENSUS

Distributed consensus is the process by which a blockchain network agrees on the state of its ledger. It is the foundation upon which blockchain achieves trustlessness and decentralization. In a system where there is no central authority, achieving consensus among a myriad of independent nodes is both complex and critical.

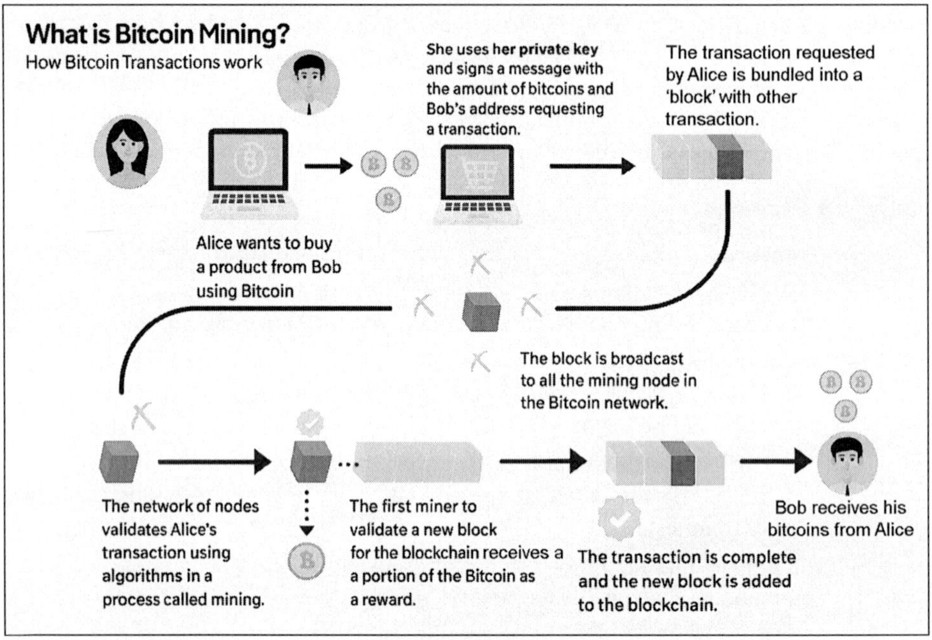

Fig. 1.3: Mining Process Flow

- **Decentralized Trust:** In a decentralized network, no single node is inherently trusted. Consensus algorithms ensure that all nodes validate transactions and agree on the ledger's state without relying on a central authority.
- **Fault Tolerance:** Consensus mechanisms are designed to tolerate a certain degree of failure or malicious behavior. Even if some nodes act unpredictably or attempt to disrupt the system, the network as a whole remains secure and reliable.

Core Properties of Consensus Algorithms

- **Consistency:** Every node must eventually agree on the same data, ensuring that the ledger is uniform across the network.

- **Liveness:** The system must continue to operate and process transactions even in the presence of failures or network delays.
- **Fault Tolerance:** Consensus algorithms must be resilient to various types of failures, including Byzantine faults where nodes may act maliciously.

Major Consensus Mechanisms

1. Proof-of-Work (PoW) as a Consensus Protocol

- **Mechanics of PoW:** PoW requires nodes (miners) to solve computational puzzles, thereby expending energy to propose a new block. The first miner to solve the puzzle broadcasts the block, and other nodes verify its correctness.
- **Security through Computation:** The heavy computational work required makes it infeasible for an attacker to alter the ledger without controlling the majority of the network's computing power.
- **Challenges and Limitations:** PoW is resource-intensive, leading to concerns about energy consumption and centralization of mining power.

2. Proof-of-Stake (PoS)

- **Mechanics of PoS:** PoS selects validators based on the amount of cryptocurrency they hold and are willing to lock up as collateral. This mechanism reduces the need for energy-intensive computations.
- **Economic Incentives:** Validators are rewarded for honest participation and penalized for malicious behavior, aligning their economic interests with network security.
- **Variants and Enhancements:** Hybrid models, Delegated Proof-of-Stake (DPoS), and other variants introduce voting and reputation systems to further refine the consensus process.

3. Byzantine Fault Tolerance (BFT)

- **Overview of BFT:** BFT algorithms are designed to handle scenarios where some nodes may act maliciously. They ensure that consensus can still be reached even when a fraction of the nodes are compromised.
- **Popular BFT Protocols:** Protocols such as Practical Byzantine Fault Tolerance (PBFT) and its derivatives have been implemented in permissioned blockchains, offering high throughput and low latency.
- **Trade-offs:** While BFT protocols provide strong guarantees of consistency, they often require a fixed and limited number of nodes, which can restrict scalability.

Consensus Algorithms in Action

Step-by-Step Consensus Process

- **Transaction Proposal:** A new transaction is broadcast to the network. Nodes validate the transaction against predefined rules.
- **Block Formation:** Valid transactions are grouped into a block. The block is then proposed by a node (miner or validator) based on the consensus mechanism in use.

- **Validation and Agreement:** The proposed block is disseminated to the network. Other nodes independently verify its validity. Only after reaching a pre-agreed threshold of approvals does the block become part of the blockchain.

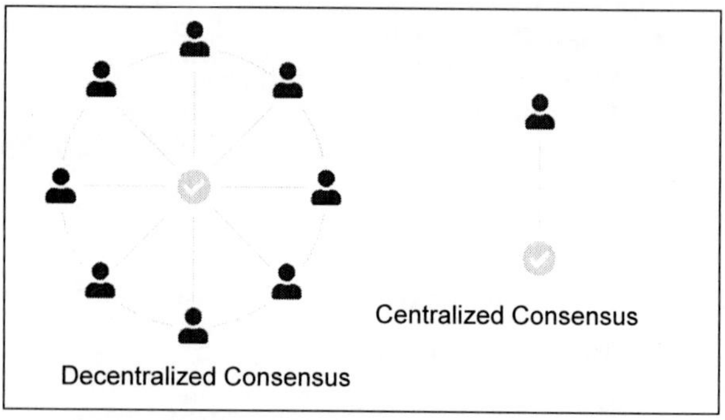

Fig. 1.4: Consensus Process in a Blockchain

- **Finality and Immutable Recording:** Once consensus is reached, the block is permanently appended to the ledger. The cryptographic links between blocks ensure that any alteration would be immediately evident.

1.5 BLOCKCHAIN EVOLUTION: 1.0, 2.0, AND 3.0

Introduction

Blockchain technology began as a groundbreaking innovation to tackle the challenges of trust, security, and decentralization in digital transactions. Over time, it has evolved from a single-purpose system to a multifaceted platform that powers a wide range of applications. The evolution of blockchain can broadly be divided into three generations: Blockchain 1.0, which laid the foundation with cryptocurrencies; Blockchain 2.0, which introduced smart contracts and decentralized applications (dApps); and Blockchain 3.0, which focuses on scalability, interoperability, and enterprise-grade solutions.

Blockchain 1.0 – The Birth of Digital Currency

- **Foundational Concepts:** Blockchain 1.0 emerged with the advent of Bitcoin in 2008, introduced by the pseudonymous Satoshi Nakamoto. This first generation of blockchain was designed to serve as a decentralized digital ledger. By recording transactions on a public, immutable ledger, it eliminated the need for a central authority, such as a bank, to validate transfers

Key Features

- **Decentralization:** In Blockchain 1.0, every transaction is recorded on a distributed network of nodes. Each node maintains a copy of the ledger, ensuring that no single entity controls the system.
- **Proof of Work (PoW):** The consensus mechanism used in Bitcoin involves miners solving complex mathematical puzzles to add new blocks. This process secures the network and helps prevent double-spending.
- **Transparency and Immutability:** Every transaction is visible to all participants and, once recorded, cannot be altered. This transparency builds trust among users.
- **Focus on Currency:** The primary use case was digital money—Bitcoin was envisioned as a means to conduct online transactions in a secure and censorship-resistant way.

- **Limitations:** While revolutionary, Blockchain 1.0 comes with inherent limitations. Its reliance on PoW means that transaction processing is energy intensive and slow, with networks like Bitcoin handling only a handful of transactions per second. Moreover, its design was solely geared toward currency transfers, leaving little room for more complex operations.

Blockchain 2.0 – Expanding Horizons with Smart Contracts

- **Evolution Beyond Currency:** Recognizing the potential of blockchain technology beyond mere digital currency, developers began to explore additional functionalities. Ethereum, launched by Vitalik Buterin in 2015, is the prime example of Blockchain 2.0. It introduced the concept of smart contracts—self-executing contracts where the terms are directly written into code and stored on the blockchain.

Key Features

- **Smart Contracts:** These are automated programs that execute when specific conditions are met. They eliminate the need for intermediaries, reduce transaction costs, and enable trustless interactions between parties.
- **Decentralized Applications (dApps):** Building on smart contracts, developers created dApps that perform various tasks—from decentralized finance (DeFi) platforms to games and supply chain management tools. This greatly expanded the utility of blockchain technology.
- **Tokenization:** Blockchain 2.0 enabled the creation of new digital assets. Tokens built on standards like ERC-20 and ERC-721 allowed for the issuance of cryptocurrencies, digital collectibles (NFTs), and even governance tokens for decentralized organizations.
- **Enhanced Flexibility:** Unlike Blockchain 1.0's narrow focus on currency, Blockchain 2.0 provides a robust framework for executing complex business logic directly on the blockchain.
- **Challenges:** Despite its expanded capabilities, Blockchain 2.0 also faces challenges. The increasing complexity of smart contracts introduces potential vulnerabilities—coding errors or security flaws can lead to significant financial losses, as seen in some high-profile hacks. Furthermore, as more applications are built on platforms like Ethereum, network congestion has led to high transaction fees and slower confirmation times, issues that have spurred ongoing efforts to improve scalability.

Blockchain 3.0 – Scalability, Interoperability, and Enterprise Adoption

- **Next-Generation Advancements:** Blockchain 3.0 aims to overcome the limitations of its predecessors by addressing scalability, improving interoperability among diverse networks, and reducing environmental impact. This generation is geared toward mainstream adoption across various industries—extending blockchain applications far beyond the financial sector.

Key Features

- **Scalability Enhancements:** One of the primary goals of Blockchain 3.0 is to handle a much higher volume of transactions. Innovations such as sharding (splitting the network into smaller, parallel-processing segments) and alternative consensus mechanisms like Proof of Stake (PoS) replace energy-intensive PoW. This shift allows for faster processing and significantly lower transaction fees.
- **Interoperability:** A major breakthrough in Blockchain 3.0 is the ability to connect disparate blockchain networks. Protocols and bridging technologies (such as those used by Polkadot and Cosmos) facilitate cross-chain communication. This means that digital assets and data can be seamlessly transferred between different blockchains, fostering a more integrated ecosystem.
- **Enhanced Security and Privacy:** With the introduction of advanced cryptographic techniques, such as zero-knowledge proofs, Blockchain 3.0 enables users to verify transactions without revealing sensitive data. This level of privacy is critical for applications in healthcare, voting, and identity management.
- **Enterprise-Grade Solutions:** Blockchain 3.0 is designed with scalability and flexibility in mind, making it well-suited for enterprise applications. Companies are now exploring its use for supply chain tracking, secure record-keeping, and even as a backbone for integrating with emerging technologies like artificial intelligence (AI) and the Internet of Things (IoT).
- **Real-World Applications:** Blockchain 3.0 is already making inroads in sectors beyond finance. In supply chain management, for instance, it can track goods from production to delivery, ensuring transparency and reducing fraud. In healthcare, blockchain platforms are used to securely store patient records and share data among authorized entities without compromising privacy. Voting systems built on Blockchain 3.0 promise to deliver tamper-proof, transparent elections, while businesses can streamline operations with secure and efficient data management systems.
- **Remaining Challenges:** While promising, Blockchain 3.0 is still an evolving technology. Interoperability standards are in development, and the security of cross-chain transactions continues to be a critical area of research. Additionally, the more complex architecture of Blockchain 3.0 systems requires careful governance to maintain decentralization without sacrificing efficiency.

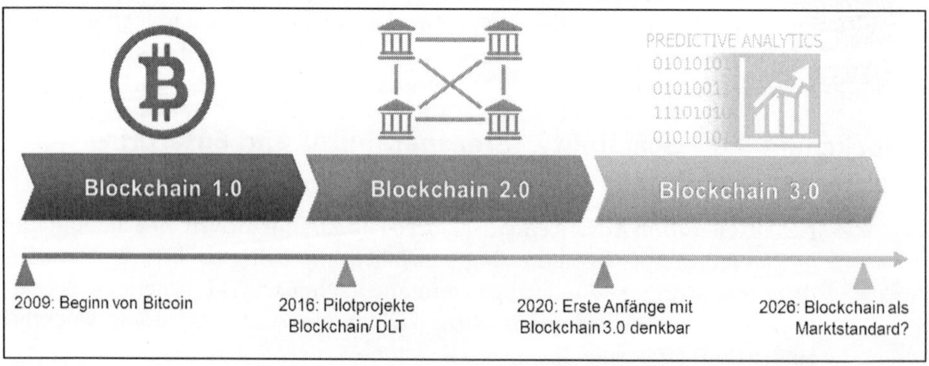

***Fig. 1.5:** Blockchain - 1.0, 2.0, and 3.0*

1.6 PRIVACY AND SECURITY ISSUES IN BLOCKCHAIN

Security Issues

- **51% Attack:** If a single entity gains control over the majority of the network's hashing power (PoW) or stake (PoS), they can manipulate the ledger (e.g., double-spending).
- **Double Spending:** The risk that a digital asset is spent more than once, mitigated by consensus algorithms.
- **Smart Contract Vulnerabilities:** Bugs or flaws in smart contract code can be exploited (e.g., DAO hack on Ethereum).
- **Sybil Attacks:** An attacker creates many pseudonymous identities to gain undue influence over the network.

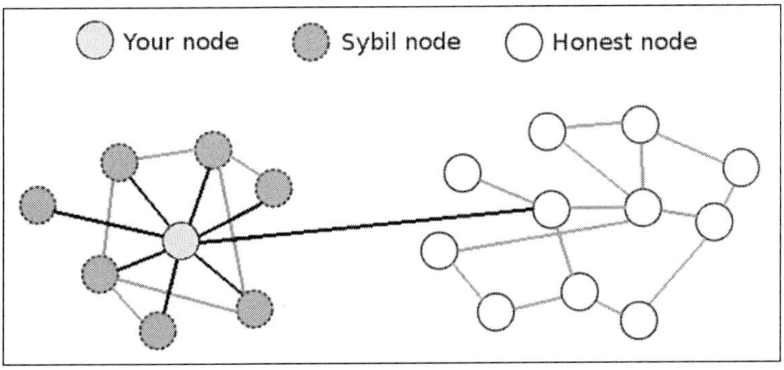

Fig. 1.6

- **Network Attacks:** Examples include Eclipse attacks, where a node is isolated from the network, and DDoS attacks targeting blockchain nodes.

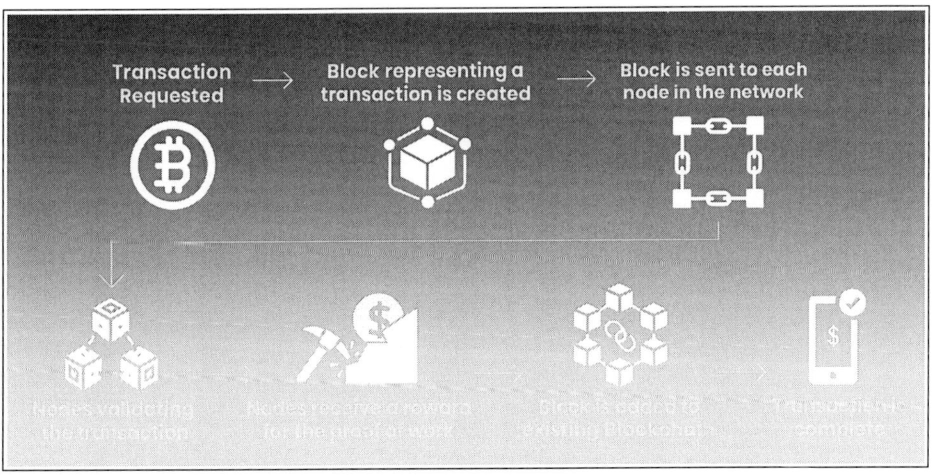

Fig. 1.7: *Privacy and Security Issues In Blockchain*

Privacy Challenges

- **Pseudonymity vs. Anonymity:** Public blockchains use pseudonymous addresses, but transaction patterns can often be linked back to real-world identities through analysis.
- **Immutable Data vs. Right to be Forgotten:** Once data is added, it cannot be removed. This immutability can conflict with privacy regulations like GDPR.

Enhancement Techniques

- **Zero-Knowledge Proofs (ZKP):** Allow one party to prove a statement is true without revealing underlying data. Used by privacy coins like Zcash.
- **Ring Signatures:** Used in Monero to obfuscate the true sender among a group.
- **Mixing and Tumbling Services:** Combine multiple transactions to mask origins, though these can also be subject to regulatory scrutiny.

Blockchain Security Issues

2

UNIT

2.1 BLOCKCHAIN RELATED ISSUES

1. Scalability

- **problem:** Blockchains war to address a large number of transactions consistent with second (TPS). for instance, Bitcoin handles ~7 TPS, and Ethereum ~30 TPS, in comparison to Visa's ~24,000 TPS.
- **cause:** every node inside the network should validate every transaction, leading to slower speeds.
- **solutions:** Layer 2 answers (e.g., Lightning community for Bitcoin), sharding, and advanced consensus algorithms (e.g., evidence of Stake).

2. Security Risks

- **51% Attack:** If a group of miners control over 50% of the network's hashing power, they could manipulate the blockchain.
- **Smart Contract Vulnerabilities:** Bugs in code can be exploited (e.g., The DAO hack on Ethereum).
- **Private Key Security:** If private keys are lost or stolen, access to the associated cryptocurrency is lost forever.

3. Energy Consumption

- **Issue:** Proof of Work (PoW) consensus mechanisms consume vast amounts of energy. Bitcoin's energy consumption is comparable to that of some countries.
- **Impact:** Environmental concerns and increased operational costs.
- **Solutions:** Transition to Proof of Stake (e.g., Ethereum's transition to Ethereum 2.0).

4. Regulatory and Legal Challenges

- **Lack of Regulation:** Unclear regulations in many countries lead to legal uncertainties.
- **Cross-border Transactions:** Jurisdiction issues arise with international transactions.
- **Compliance Issues:** Challenges with Anti-Money Laundering (AML) and Know Your Customer (KYC) requirements.

5. Privacy Concerns

- **Transparency vs. Privacy**: Blockchain's transparent nature conflicts with user privacy.
- **Traceability**: Transactions are traceable, which can compromise anonymity.
- **Solutions**: Privacy-focused cryptocurrencies (e.g., Monero) and ZK-SNARKs (Zero-Knowledge Proofs).

6. Interoperability Issues

- **Problem**: Blockchains operate in silos, limiting data and asset transfers across different networks.
- **Impact**: Reduced efficiency and usability.
- **Solutions**: Cross-chain bridges, interoperability protocols (e.g., Polkadot, Cosmos).

7. User Experience and Adoption Barriers

- **Complexity:** Difficult for non-technical users to understand and use.
- **Usability Issues:** Managing private keys and wallets is cumbersome.
- **Adoption:** Limited acceptance by businesses and users due to volatility and complexity.

8. Economic and Market Risks

- **Volatility**: High price volatility in cryptocurrencies affects investment stability.
- **Speculative Investments**: Many tokens have no intrinsic value, leading to market bubbles.
- **Scams and Fraud**: ICO scams and Ponzi schemes are common in the unregulated crypto market.

9. Governance Challenges

- **Decentralization vs. Governance**: Managing changes or upgrades in decentralized systems is challenging.
- **Forks**: Disagreements within the community lead to hard forks (e.g., Bitcoin and Bitcoin Cash split).
- **Power Concentration**: Mining centralization and influence of large stakeholders conflict with decentralization principles.

Addressing these challenges requires technological advancements, regulatory clarity, and a balanced approach to security, privacy, and governance.

2.2 HIGHER-LEVEL LANGUAGE (SOLIDITY) RELATED ISSUES

Solidity, the primary programming language for developing smart contracts on Ethereum, offers powerful functionalities but also comes with several challenges and risks. Here are the main issues:

1. Security Vulnerabilities

a. Reentrancy Attack

- **Description:** Occurs when an external contract repeatedly calls back into the calling contract before the first function execution completes, potentially draining funds.
- **Example:** The DAO hack in 2016.
- **Prevention:**
  - Use the Checks-Effects-Interactions pattern.
  - Implement reentrancy guards (reentrancyGuard modifier).

Contract A	Contract B (Attacker)
1. Call Function --------->	2. Call back to A's function before completion
3. Repeat Withdrawal ------->	4. Drain Funds

b. Unchecked Call Return Values

- **Description:** Low-level calls (call(), delegate call()) return a Boolean status. If unchecked, failures may go unnoticed, leading to security risks.
- **Prevention:** Always check the return value using require() or assert().

call() -> false (Failed)

↓

No Revert (Funds Lost)

2. Gas Optimization Issues

- **High Gas Costs:** Complex logic or excessive storage operations lead to expensive transactions.
- **Gas Limit Exceeded:** If gas usage exceeds the block gas limit, the transaction fails.
- **Optimization Techniques:**
  - Use call data instead of memory for function arguments.
  - Pack storage variables to reduce storage slots.
  - Minimize loops and external contract calls.

3. Smart Contract Upgradability

- **Issue:** Once deployed, smart contracts are immutable, making bug fixes and feature upgrades challenging.
- **Workaround:** Use the Proxy Contract pattern, where a proxy delegates calls to an implementation contract.
- **Risks:** Improper upgrade logic can introduce security vulnerabilities.

4. Access Control Issues

- **Description:** Incorrect implementation of access control allows unauthorized users to execute sensitive functions.

- **Example:** Missing only Owner modifier or misconfigured roles.
- **Prevention:** Use Ownable or Access Control from Open Zeppelin.

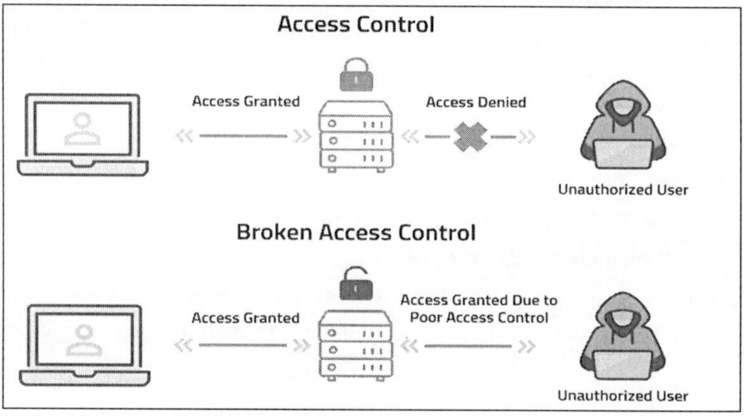

Fig. 2.1: Access Control Issues

5. Randomness Vulnerabilities

- **Issue**: Using block timestamp or block hash for randomness is insecure as miners can manipulate them.
- **Impact:** Predictable outcomes in lotteries or games.
- **Solution:** Use off-chain oracles like Chain link VRF for secure randomness.

6. Floating Point Precision Issues

- **Issue:** Solidity does not support floating-point numbers, leading to precision errors in calculations.
- **Example:** 3 / 2 = 1 instead of 1.5.
- **Solution:** Use fixed-point libraries or scale values to integers (e.g., using 10^{18} as amultiplier).

7. External Contract Dependencies

- **Issue:** Reliance on external contracts increases the attack surface, especially if they are compromised.
- **Example:** Dependency on an Oracle that is attacked or manipulated.
- **Solution:** Use trusted and verified contracts (e.g., Open Zeppelin) and minimize external calls.

Diagram

Contract A

↓

External Contract

↓

Compromised / Malicious

8. Denial of Service (DoS) Attacks

- **Description:** An attacker prevents users from accessing contract functionality.
- **Example:** DoS with gas limit by making a loop expensive or blocking withdrawals by becoming the largest receiver.
- **Prevention:** Limit loop iterations and use pull-over-push pattern for payments.

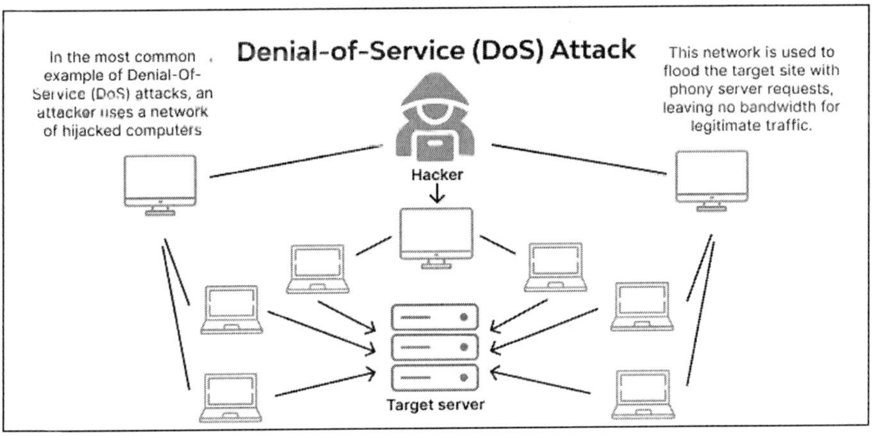

Fig. 2.2: Denial of Service (DoS) Attack

9. Time Manipulation

- **Issue:** Miners can manipulate block timestamp, affecting time-dependent smart contracts.
- **Example:** Miners delay transactions to win time-based games.
- **Solution:** Avoid using timestamps for critical logic; use block numbers instead.

Block timestamp

↓

Manipulated by Miner

10. Poor Coding Practices

- **Issue**: Writing unoptimized or poorly structured code increases gas costs and security risks.
- **Examples:** Unused variables, inefficient loops, and complex conditionals.
- **Solution:** Follow best practices, use linters, and perform code audits.

Poor Code Quality

↓

High Gas Costs / Vulnerabilities

To mitigate these issues, developers should follow best practices, use security libraries, perform audits, and stay updated with the latest Solidity features and community guidelines.

2.3 EVM BYTECODE RELATED ISSUES

(Ethereum Virtual Machine) Bytecode is the low-level representation of smart contracts deployed on the Ethereum blockchain. It is executed by the EVM, enabling decentralized application logic. However, working with EVM bytecode presents several challenges and security risks. Here are the key issues:

1. Security Vulnerabilities

a. Reentrancy Attack

- **Description**: EVM's call mechanism allows contracts to call external functions, potentially enabling recursive calls before state changes are finalized.
- **Impact**: Funds can be drained by repeatedly calling the withdrawal function.
- **Prevention**:
  - Use Checks-Effects-Interactions pattern.

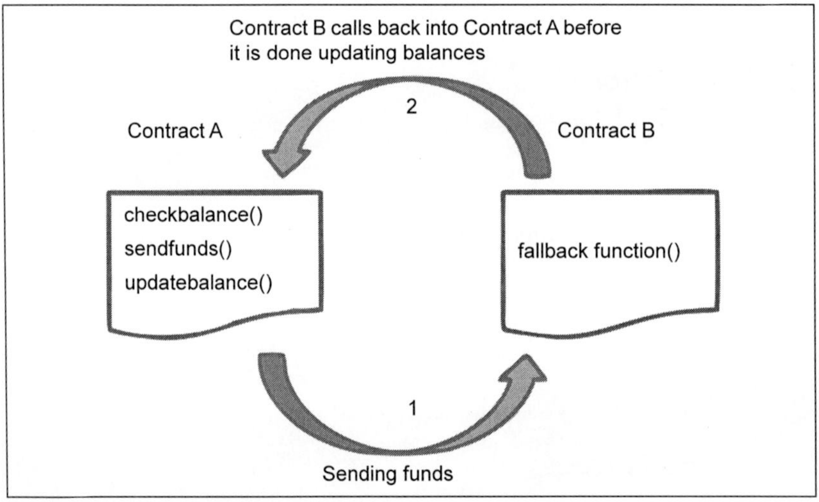

Fig. 2.3: *Implement reentrancy guards*

b. Delegatecall Injection

- **Description**: DELEGATECALL executes code in the context of the calling contract, affecting its state. If improperly used, malicious code can take control.
- **Impact**: Attackers can overwrite contract storage, changing ownership or draining funds.
- **Prevention**:
  - Validate input addresses.
  - Use trusted contracts only for DELEGATECALL.

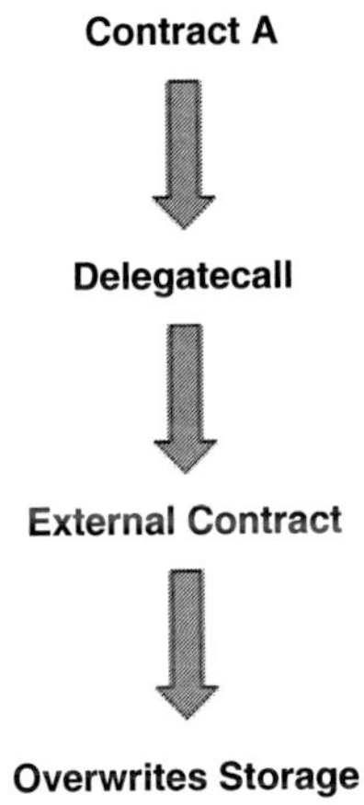

c. Short Address Attack

- **Description**: Occurs when the input data is shorter than expected, causing incorrect parameter parsing. This exploits EVM's padding mechanism.
- **Impact**: Attackers manipulate token transfers or other transactions.
- **Prevention**:
  - Validate input data length.
  - Use OpenZeppelin's SafeERC20 library.

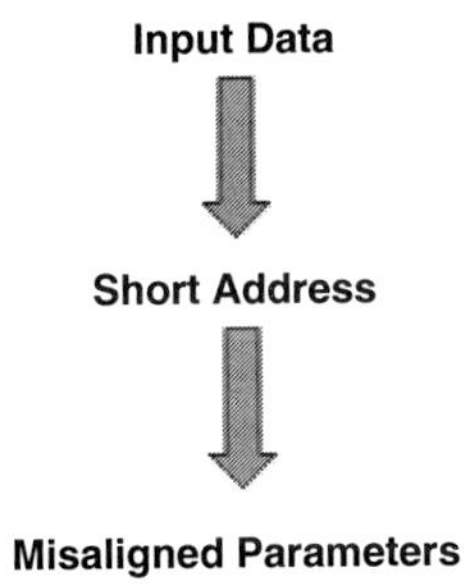

2. Gas Optimization Issues

a. High Gas Costs

- **Description**: Inefficient bytecode can consume excessive gas, making transactions expensive.
- **Cause**:
  - Redundant opcodes.
  - Complex loops and storage operations.
- **Optimization Techniques**:
  - Optimize storage access and packing.
  - Minimize SSTORE and SLOAD operations.
  - Use fewer computational steps.

b. Gas Limit Exceeded

- **Description**: When gas usage exceeds the block's gas limit, the transaction fails.
- **Cause**: Complex logic or unbounded loops.
- **Prevention**: Optimize contract logic and avoid unbounded loops.

3. Opcode-Level Vulnerabilities

a. SELFDESTRUCT Abuse

- **Description**: SELFDESTRUCT removes contract bytecode and sends the remaining ether to a specified address.
- **Impact**: Attackers can force ether into contracts, breaking invariant checks.
- **Prevention**: Avoid balance-dependent logic and handle unexpected ether.

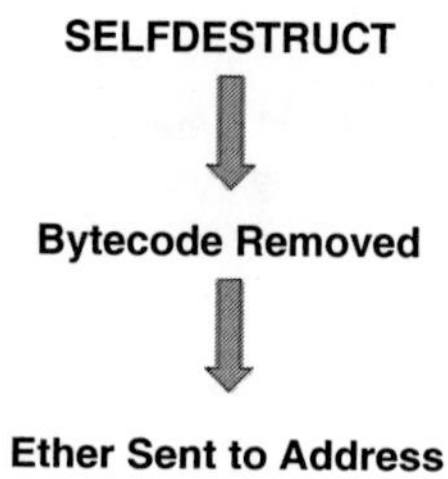

b. Unintended Delegatecall Behaviour

- **Description**: DELEGATECALL executes external code but maintains the context of the calling contract. Malicious code can alter storage variables.
- **Impact**: Attackers gain control over contract state variables.
- **Prevention**: Use trusted contracts and validate external addresses.

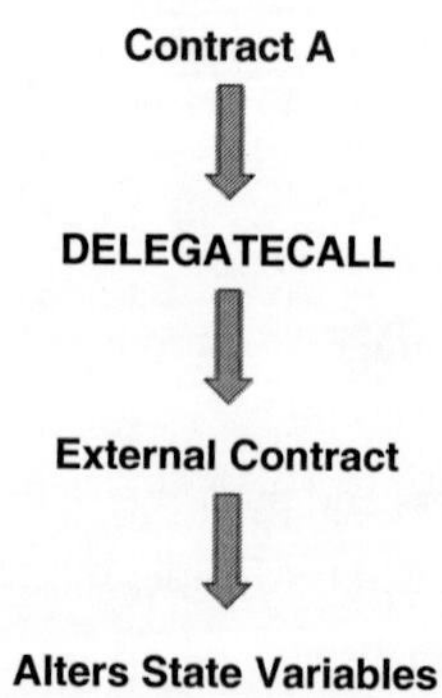

4. Immutable Bytecode Issues

- **Description**: Once deployed, bytecode is immutable. Bugs or vulnerabilities cannot be fixed directly.
- **Impact**: Critical bugs remain exploitable, leading to loss of funds or functionality.
- **Workaround**: Use proxy contracts for upgradability.

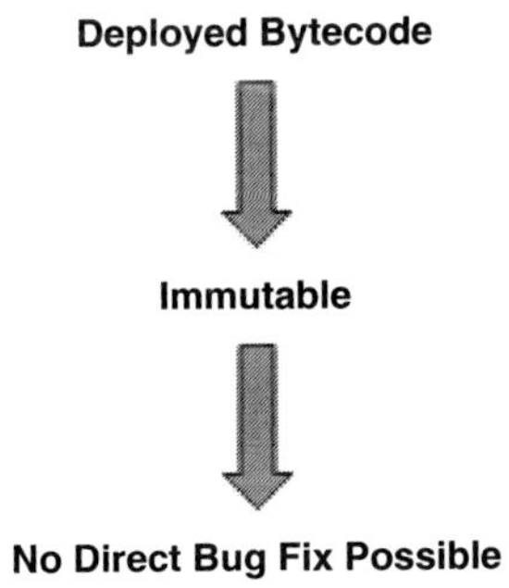

5. Lack of Debugging and Readability

- **Description**: Bytecode is difficult to read and debug as it lacks high-level context and variable names.
- **Impact**: Complex error tracing and increased debugging time.
- **Solution**:
    - Use source maps and debugging tools like Remix and Hardhat.
    - Write well-documented Solidity code for better traceability.

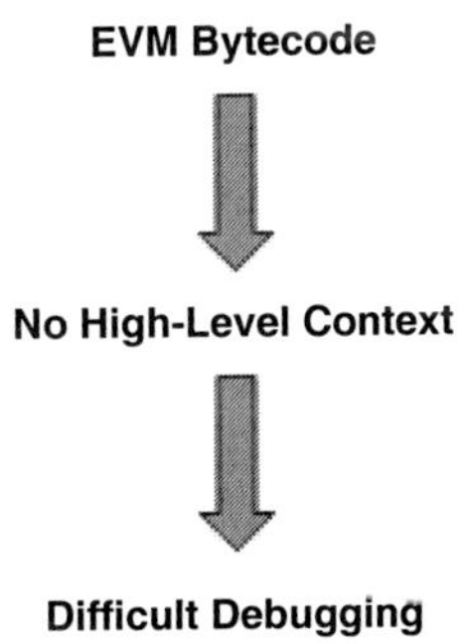

6. Inconsistent Opcode Costs

- **Description**: Gas costs for opcodes are periodically adjusted (e.g., Istanbul update), potentially breaking previously functional contracts.
- **Impact**: Contracts may fail or become uneconomical to use.
- **Solution**: Write gas-efficient contracts and stay updated with EIPs (Ethereum Improvement Proposals).

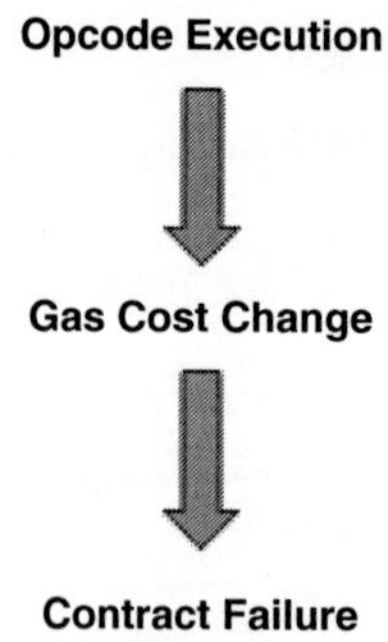

Developers must adopt best practices, including security audits, gas optimization techniques, and proxy patterns for upgradability. Staying informed about EVM updates and utilizing robust debugging tools are essential for secure and efficient smart contract development.

2.4 REAL-LIFE ATTACKS ON BLOCKCHAIN APPLICATIONS/ SMART CONTRACTS

Blockchain applications and smart contracts offer decentralized, transparent, and secure systems. However, they are not immune to attacks. Here are some notable real-life incidents, their impact, and how they could have been prevented.

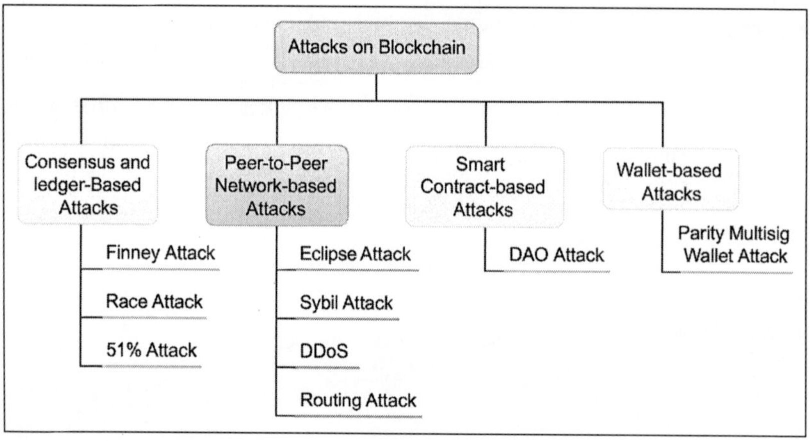

Fig. 2.4

1. The DAO Hack (2016)

- **Description**: One of the largest Ethereum hacks, where a vulnerability in a smart contract allowed an attacker to drain about **$60 million worth of Ether**.
- **Attack Vector**: **Reentrancy Attack**
  - The smart contract allowed recursive calls to the withdrawal function before updating the user's balance.
- **Impact**: Ethereum hard-forked to restore stolen funds, leading to the creation of Ethereum (ETH) and Ethereum Classic (ETC).

- **Prevention**:
  - Use the Checks-Effects-Interactions pattern.
  - Implement reentrancy guards (reentrancyGuard modifier).

Diagram

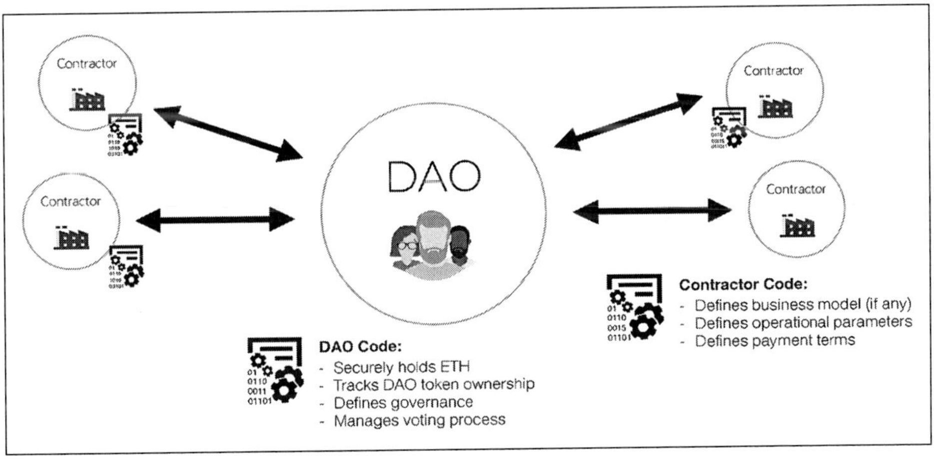

Fig. 2.5

2.Parity Multisig Wallet Hack (2017)

- **Description**: Two separate incidents due to flawed smart contract coding in the Parity Wallet library.
  - **First Incident**: **$30 million** was stolen due to a bug allowing anyone to become the owner and drain funds.
  - **Second Incident**: **$300 million** worth of Ether was frozen when a user accidentally triggered the selfdestruct function.
- **Attack Vector**:
  - **First**: Insecure initWallet function allowing ownership takeover.
  - **Second**: Uninitialized library contract vulnerability.
- **Impact**: Funds were permanently lost due to immutability of blockchain contracts.
- **Prevention**:
  - Proper initialization checks and access control.
  - Avoid using selfdestruct without stringent checks.

3. Mt. Gox Exchange Hack (2014)

- **Description**: One of the earliest and largest Bitcoin exchange hacks. About **850,000 BTC** were stolen due to security lapses and transaction malleability.
- **Attack Vector: Transaction Malleability**
  - Attackers altered transaction hashes before confirmation, enabling double spending.
- **Impact**: The exchange declared bankruptcy, and users lost significant amounts of Bitcoin.

- **Prevention**:
  - Implement better transaction ID verification.
  - Use Segregated Witness (SegWit) to fix transaction malleability

Fig. 2.6: *Mt. Gox Exchange Hack (2014)*

4. Ronin Bridge Hack (2022)

- **Description**: Hackers exploited the bridge between **Axie Infinity's Ronin Network** and Ethereum, stealing **$620 million** in Ether and USDC.
- **Attack Vector**: **Private Key Compromise & Insufficient Validator Security**
  - Attackers gained control of five out of nine validators to authorize withdrawals.
- **Impact**: One of the largest crypto heists, shaking confidence in cross-chain bridges.
- **Prevention**:
  - Increase the number of validators required for consensus.
  - Use multi-signature wallets and hardware security modules.

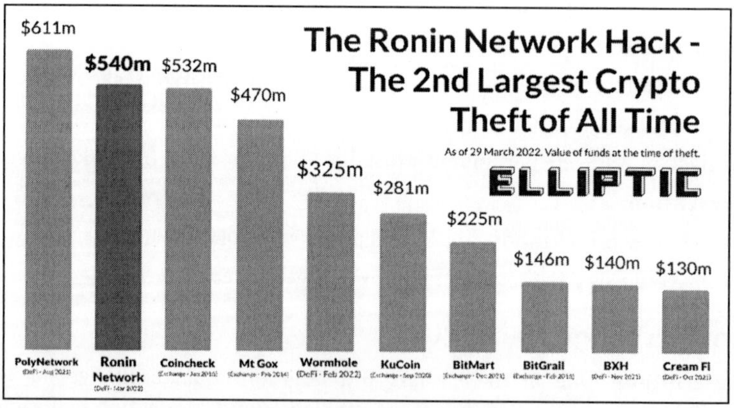

Fig. 2.7: *Ronin Bridge Hack*

5. Finance Exploits (2021)

- **Description**: Multiple flash loan attacks on Cream Finance, resulting in losses exceeding **$130 million**.

- **Attack Vector: Flash Loan Exploit & Price Oracle Manipulation**
  - Attackers manipulated token prices using flash loans, allowing them to drain liquidity.
- **Impact**: Users lost funds, and the platform's credibility was severely affected.
- **Prevention**:
  - Use decentralized and time-weighted price oracles.
  - Implement reentrancy guards and proper validation checks.

6. Poly Network Hack (2021)

- **Description**: Exploited a vulnerability in the Poly Network's cross-chain bridge, leading to **$610 million** theft. The hacker later returned the funds.
- **Attack Vector: Cross-Chain Messaging Flaw**
  - Improper access control in cross-chain communication contracts.
- **Impact**: Largest DeFi hack by value; highlighted security risks in cross-chain bridges.
- **Prevention**:
  - Strengthen access control and validation logic.
  - Conduct thorough security audits and testing for cross-chain protocols.

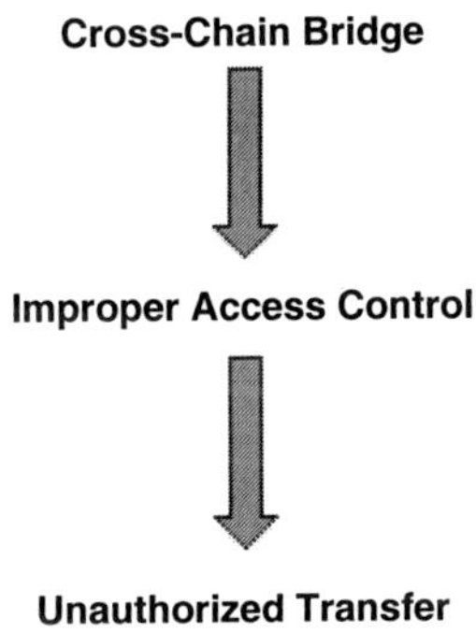

7. bZx Protocol Exploits (2020)

- **Description**: Exploited multiple times using flash loans, resulting in a combined loss of **$8.1 million**.
- **Attack Vector: Oracle Manipulation & Flash Loans**
  - Attackers manipulated the price feed, enabling them to profit from leveraged trades.
- **Impact**: Repeated hacks damaged the platform's reputation.
- **Prevention**:
  - Use decentralized oracles for accurate price feeds.
  - Implement limits on price changes within short time frames.

These real-life attacks highlight critical security challenges in blockchain and smart contract applications. Common attack vectors include:

- **Reentrancy** (DAO Hack)
- **Access Control Flaws** (Parity Wallet)
- **Transaction Malleability** (Mt. Gox)
- **Private Key Compromise** (Ronin Bridge)
- **Price Oracle Manipulation** (Cream Finance, bZx)
- **Cross-Chain Communication Flaws** (Poly Network)

2.5 TRUSTED EXECUTION ENVIRONMENTS

Trusted Execution Environments (TEEs) are secure areas within a device's main processor that isolate code execution and data to ensure confidentiality and integrity. They are used in blockchain systems to enhance security by securely managing private keys, confidential data, and off-chain computations.

What are Trusted Execution Environments (TEEs)?

- **Definition**: A TEE is a secure enclave within a device's processor that provides a protected area for sensitive computations.
- **Purpose in Blockchain**:
  - Secure management of **private keys** and **digital signatures**.
  - Confidential off-chain computations, preserving data privacy.
  - **Oracle services** to provide secure off-chain data feeds.
- **Popular Implementations**:
  - Intel SGX (Software Guard Extensions)
  - ARM TrustZone
  - AMD SEV (Secure Encrypted Virtualization)

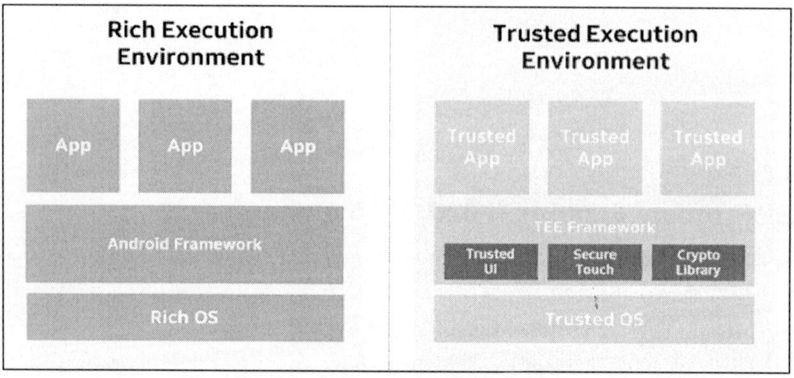

Fig. 2.8: *TEE Architecture*

Role of TEEs in Blockchain

1. Secure Key Management

- Store private keys securely within the TEE, preventing exposure even if the OS is compromised.
- Used in wallets, digital signatures, and transaction validation.

2. Confidential Smart Contracts

- Enable private smart contract execution off-chain while ensuring data integrity.
- Example: **Secret Network** uses TEEs for privacy-preserving smart contracts.

3. Secure Oracles

- TEEs provide a trusted environment for oracle nodes to fetch and verify off-chain data.
- Example: **Town Crier** uses Intel SGX to securely fetch HTTPS data for Ethereum.

Limitations of TEEs in Blockchain

1. Centralization Risk

- Relying on proprietary hardware (e.g., Intel SGX) introduces centralization, conflicting with blockchain's decentralized nature.

2. Scalability Concerns

- TEEs have limited computational resources, affecting performance for large-scale decentralized applications.

3. Regulatory Compliance

- TEEs often operate under jurisdiction-specific export control regulations, impacting cross-border blockchain applications.

Intentionally Left Blank!

Smart Contracts

3

UNIT

3.1 DEFINITION AND NEED

Definition of Smart Contracts

- A **Smart Contract** is a self-executing contract where the agreement terms are written into code and automatically executed when predefined conditions are met. They are deployed on blockchain platforms like Ethereum.
- **How it Works:**
  - The contract automatically triggers actions (e.g., transferring funds or assets) once conditions are fulfilled, eliminating the need for intermediaries.
- **Example:**
  - A buyer sends payment, and when the payment is verified, the contract automatically releases the product.

Need for Smart Contracts

1. Efficiency

Automates processes, reducing delays associated with manual contract execution.

2. Cost-Effectiveness

Eliminates intermediaries (e.g., lawyers, brokers), cutting transaction costs.

3. Trust and Transparency

Blockchain ensures all contract terms are visible and immutable, building trust among parties.

4. Security

Blockchain encryption and decentralization make smart contracts secure from tampering.

5. Decentralization

No central authority is needed, reducing reliance on third-party entities.

6. Speed

Execution is near-instantaneous once conditions are met, unlike traditional contracts that take longer.

7. Reduced Errors

Automation reduces human error in contract execution.

8. Improved Accountability

The blockchain provides an auditable record, ensuring accountability and transparency.

3.2 SMART CONTRACTS FEATURES

1. Automation

Once deployed, smart contracts automatically execute actions based on predefined conditions, eliminating manual intervention.

2. Transparency

The terms of the contract are visible to all participants, ensuring clarity and reducing fraud.

3. Security

Blockchain's cryptographic techniques ensure that data and transactions are secure and tamper-proof.

4. Immutability

Once deployed, the terms of the smart contract cannot be changed, ensuring consistency.

5. Speed

Transactions are processed almost instantly when conditions are met, compared to traditional methods.

6. Cost-Effectiveness

Eliminates intermediaries, reducing transaction costs significantly.

7. Trustless Transactions

Parties don't need to trust each other because the contract is enforced automatically by the blockchain.

8. Flexibility

Smart contracts can be customized for various industries, such as finance, insurance, or real estate.

9. Self-Execution

The contract executes itself when the conditions are satisfied, ensuring automated execution.

10. Reduced Human Error

The automation and blockchain system minimize the risk of human mistakes in executing the contract.

3.3 LIFE CYCLE OF A SMART CONTRACT

The life cycle of a smart contract refers to the series of stages it goes through from creation to deployment and interaction. Below are the key phases:

1. Design and Planning

- **Objective Definition:** The purpose and functionality of the smart contract are defined, such as automating a specific process or handling transactions.
- **Specifications:** Detailed design of the contract, including its logic, rules, and how it will interact with users or other smart contracts.
- **Security Considerations:** Analyzing and preparing for potential security threats (e.g., reentrancy attacks, overflow/underflow).

2. Development

- **Code Writing:** The smart contract is written in a programming language such as Solidity (Ethereum), Vyper, or Rust (Solana).
- **Internal Testing:** The initial code is tested internally by the development team in a controlled environment to ensure logic correctness.
- **Code Review:** Peer reviews of the code are performed to identify any vulnerabilities or inefficiencies.

3. Testing

- **Unit Testing:** Testing of individual components or functions to verify their correctness.
- **Integration Testing:** Testing how the contract interacts with other contracts or external systems (e.g., oracles, other smart contracts).
- **Test Networks (Testnets):** The contract is deployed to a testnet (e.g., Rinkeby, Ropsten for Ethereum) for real-world simulations without risking real assets.
- **Security Audits:** External auditors may review the code to find potential vulnerabilities and bugs that developers missed.

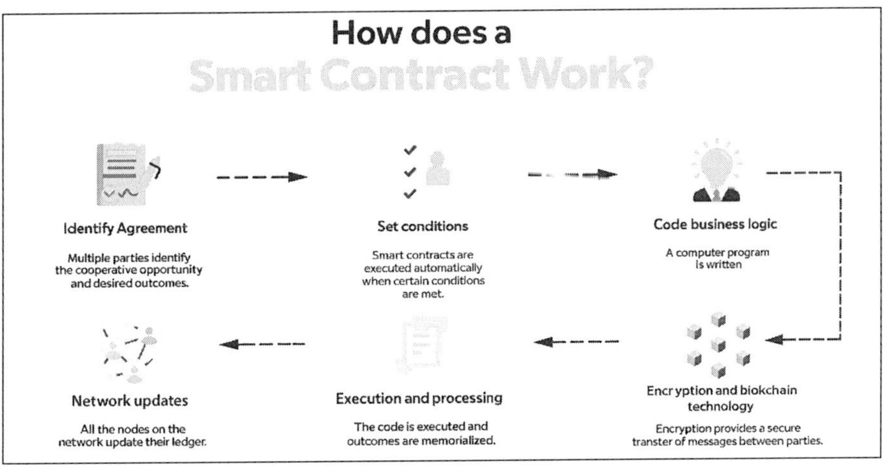

Fig. 3.1

4. Interaction

- **User Interaction:** Users or other contracts interact with the smart contract by calling its functions (e.g., sending transactions, invoking specific contract methods).
- **Events and Logs:** Smart contracts can emit events and logs, which can be captured and processed by external applications or services.
- **Transaction Processing:** The smart contract processes transactions based on the provided inputs, executes the logic, and updates the blockchain state.

5. Upgrades and Maintenance (if applicable)

- **Upgradable Contracts:** Some smart contracts include mechanisms for upgrading (e.g., proxy contracts) to fix bugs or introduce new features after deployment.
- **Contract Replacement:** If upgrades are not possible, a new version of the contract may be deployed, and users are directed to interact with the new contract.
- **Bug Fixes:** Any discovered vulnerabilities or issues require patches, but these are only possible if the contract design allows for upgradability.

6. Termination or Archival

- **Contract Expiry:** Some smart contracts are designed with an expiry date or a condition for termination (e.g., the contract might have a specific end block or time).
- **Self-Destruction:** The contract may have a self-destruct function, which removes it from the blockchain when no longer needed.
- **Archiving Data:** If the contract is no longer active, the data it interacted with may be archived, but the contract code itself remains on the blockchain, providing an immutable record.

3.4 INTRODUCTION TO ETHEREUM HIGHER-LEVEL LANGUAGES

Ethereum is one of the most popular blockchain platforms for decentralized applications (dApps). Smart contracts on Ethereum can be written using higher-level programming languages. These languages abstract away the complexity of working directly with the Ethereum Virtual Machine (EVM) bytecode, making it easier to build robust and efficient smart contracts.

Here are the key aspects of Ethereum's higher-level languages:

1. What are Higher-Level Languages?

- **Definition:** Higher-level languages are programming languages that are designed to be more user-friendly and easier to write, read, and understand. They provide abstractions that handle much of the low-level functionality for developers.
- **Purpose in Ethereum:** They make it easier for developers to write smart contracts without needing to understand the low-level bytecode and assembly language of the Ethereum Virtual Machine (EVM).

2. Key Higher-Level Languages for Ethereum

Solidity

- **Most Popular:** Solidity is the most widely used language for writing smart contracts on Ethereum.
- **Syntax:** It is similar to JavaScript, which makes it easier for developers with web development experience.
- **Features:**
  - Contract-oriented programming model.
  - Supports inheritance, libraries, and complex user-defined types.
  - Strong typing system to reduce errors.
- **Use Cases:** Primarily used for decentralized applications (dApps), tokens (ERC-20, ERC-721), and decentralized finance (DeFi) protocols.

Vyper

- **Security-Focused:** Vyper is designed to be more secure and auditable compared to Solidity.
- **Minimalistic Syntax:** It has fewer features compared to Solidity to reduce complexity and security risks.
- **Features:**
  - Simpler, more readable code.
  - Focus on security and transparency.
  - Less prone to complex bugs and vulnerabilities.
- **Use Cases:** Used in scenarios where security is the top priority, such as in financial smart contracts.

Lisp-based Languages (e.g., LLL, Bamboo)

- **Low-Level Control:** Languages like LLL (Low-Level Lisp-like Language) and Bamboo provide more low-level control over the bytecode and EVM.
- **Features:**
  - Direct interaction with the EVM, offering optimized performance and reduced gas costs.
  - Generally more complex and harder to work with than Solidity or Vyper.
- **Use Cases:** Preferred for performance-critical applications where developers need granular control over the contract's execution.

3. Characteristics of Ethereum Higher-Level Languages

- **Abstraction:** These languages offer a higher level of abstraction than raw EVM bytecode, allowing developers to focus on logic rather than implementation details.
- **Ease of Use:** They are designed to be more developer-friendly with familiar syntax and tools, making it easier to create, test, and deploy smart contracts.

- **Smart Contract Specific Features:** They include language constructs that are tailored for Ethereum's decentralized environment, such as managing gas, state changes, and interactions with other contracts.

4. Solidity – A Deep Dive

- **Contract Structure:** A Solidity contract consists of functions, state variables, events, and modifiers.
    - **State Variables:** Variables that store data on the blockchain.
    - **Functions:** The logic of the contract, which can be public or private.
    - **Modifiers:** Functions that are used to change the behavior of other functions.
    - **Events:** Used to log actions on the blockchain for external observers.
- **Gas Management:** Solidity provides tools to manage gas, ensuring that transactions remain efficient and cost-effective.
- **Inheritance:** Solidity allows smart contracts to inherit the properties of other contracts, promoting code reuse and modularity.
- **Libraries:** Libraries are collections of functions that can be reused across multiple contracts.

5. Smart Contract Deployment

- **Compilation:** High-level language code is compiled into EVM bytecode, which is executed by the Ethereum nodes.
- **Testing:** It's crucial to test the smart contracts on testnets (like Rinkeby, Ropsten) before deploying them to the Ethereum mainnet.
- **Security Audits:** Smart contracts written in higher-level languages like Solidity need to undergo thorough security audits to avoid vulnerabilities like reentrancy attacks and overflow/underflow errors.

6. The Role of Gas in Ethereum Contracts

- **Gas Calculation:** Higher-level languages like Solidity include built-in gas estimation tools. Gas is used to pay for computations on the Ethereum network.
- **Gas Optimization:** Solidity developers need to optimize their code to minimize gas usage to keep the contract execution cost-efficient.

7. Advantages of Using Higher-Level Languages

- **Faster Development:** These languages simplify smart contract development, reducing the learning curve.
- **Community Support:** Solidity, for example, has a large and active community, offering numerous tutorials, tools, and libraries to speed up development.
- **Security and Transparency:** Vyper focuses on reducing complexity, making it easier to find and fix bugs.

8. Challenges and Considerations

- **Learning Curve:** Although higher-level languages are easier than raw EVM bytecode, they still require specialized knowledge of blockchain principles, gas optimization, and security.

- **Security Risks:** While higher-level languages provide abstractions, they can still introduce vulnerabilities if not properly written and tested.
- **Performance Issues:** Higher-level languages may not be as optimized as low-level languages for performance-critical applications, especially in terms of gas consumption.

3.5 BUILDING A SIMPLE SMART CONTRACT WITH SOLIDITY

1. Setting Up the Development Environment

To write and deploy smart contracts, you need a development environment. Some common tools include:

- **Remix IDE** (browser-based IDE for Solidity).
- **Truffle** and **Hardhat** (frameworks for Ethereum development).

2. Writing the Smart Contract Code

Here's an example of a simple smart contract in Solidity:

```
solidity
contract SimpleStorage { uint256 private storedData;
constructor(uint256 initialValue) { storedData = initialValue;
}
function set(uint256 x) public { storedData = x;
}
function get() public view returns (uint256) { return storedData;
}
}
```

- **State Variable**: storedDataholds the value.
- **Constructor**: Initializes storedDatawith an initial value.
- **Functions**:
  - **set:** Stores a new value in storedData.
  - **get:** Returns the stored value.

3. Testing the Smart Contract

- In **Remix IDE**, compile and deploy the contract using **JavaScript VM** or connect to a testnet.
- Test the contract by calling setto store a value and getto retrieve it.

4. Deploying the Contract

- Deploy the contract to an Ethereum network (Mainnet or Testnet) using MetaMask.
- **Gas Fees**: Gas fees are required for deployment and interactions.

5. Interacting with the Contract

- **Call set(42): Store the value 42 in storedData.**
- **Call get(): Retrieve the stored value.**

6. Security Considerations

- **Reentrancy Attacks**: Ensure state changes occur before external calls.
- **Overflow/Underflow**: Solidity version 0.8.x handles this automatically.
- **Access Control**: Ensure proper permission checks are in place.

7. Contract Upgrades

- **Smart contracts are immutable.**
- **Use** Proxy contracts **for upgradeability.**

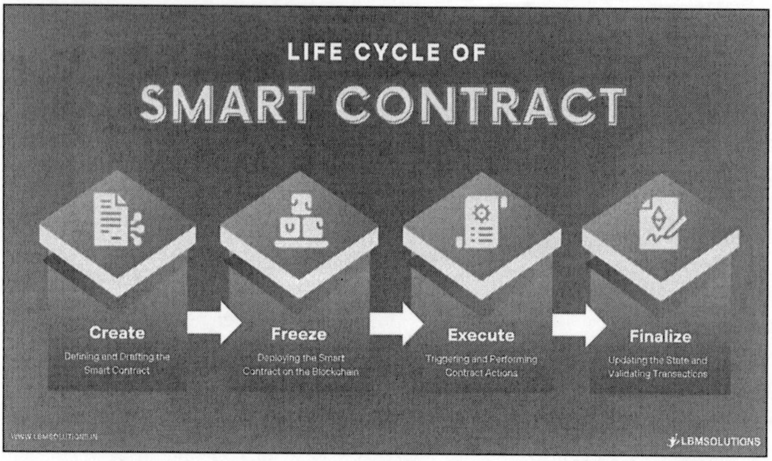

Fig. 3.2

3.6 SMART CONTRACT CREATION

A smart contract, also known as a crypto contract, is a computer software that, under specific circumstances, directly and automatically regulates the transfer of digital assets between the parties. A smart contract enforces the agreement automatically and functions similarly to a traditional contract. Smart contracts are programs that run precisely as their developers have configured, written, and programmed them. Smart contracts are enforceable by code, just like regular contracts are by law.

In order to move wealth from one individual to another, the bitcoin network was the first to use smart contracts of any kind.

Basic conditions are used by the smart contract in question, such as verifying that the sender account genuinely has the amount of value to be transferred.

3.6.1 Characteristics of Smart Contracts

Some crucial features of a smart contract are as follows:

- **Distributed:** Every member of the network is assured to have a copy of the smart contract's terms, which are unchangeable by any party. Every node linked to the network distributes and replicates a smart contract.
- **Deterministic:** Only when the necessary criteria are satisfied will smart contracts carry out the tasks for which they were created. Regardless of who executes the smart contract, the end result will remain the same.

- **Immutable:** Once a smart contract is launched, it cannot be undone; removal is only possible if the functionality has already been put into place.
- **Autonomy:** No outside parties are involved. You create the contract, and the parties share it. Because there are no middlemen, bullying is reduced and the parties concerned have complete authority. Additionally, every node on the network maintains and executes the smart contract, taking all control away from any one party.
- **Customizable:** Before being deployed, smart contracts can be altered, or more accurately, customized, to do the tasks that the user desires. Transparent: Because smart contracts are always kept on a blockchain, a publicly distributed ledger, the code is accessible to everyone, regardless of whether they are smart contract participants or not.
- **Transparent:** Smart contracts are always maintained on a public distributed ledger known as blockchain, so the code is available to everyone, regardless of whether they are smart contract participants.
- **Trustless:** Third parties are not obliged to assess if the necessary requirements are met or to confirm the process's integrity.
- **Self-verifying:** Since there are automated possibilities, these are self-verifying.
- **Self-enforcing:** When all requirements and guidelines are fulfilled, these are self-enforcing.

3.6.2 Smart Contract Types

1. Smart Legal Contract

Smart contracts have legal protections. The structure they adhere to is similar to that found in contracts: "If this occurs, then this will occur." Since legal smart contracts are maintained on blockchain and cannot be changed, they offer greater transparency between contracting entities than traditional paperwork. Digital signatures are used by the parties to complete contracts. Smart legal contracts might work independently if specific requirements are fulfilled, such as paying a debt by a specified deadline. Serious legal repercussions could result from stakeholders' noncompliance.

2. Decentralized Autonomous Organizations (DAOs)

DAOs are democratic organizations that have the ability to vote thanks to smart contracts. A blockchain-based organization with a common objective under collective control is known as a decentralized autonomous organization, or DAO. The terms president and executive do not exist. Rather, the contract's code incorporates blockchain-based concepts that regulate the organization's operations and asset distribution. VitaDAO is one instance of this type of smart contract, which leverages technology to support a community devoted to scientific research.

3. Application Logic Contracts

Application logic contracts, or ALCs, are made comprised of application-based code that typically maintains synchronization with several other blockchain contracts. It enables device-to-device communication, including the Internet of Things and blockchain integration. Unlike other types of smart contracts, these are signed between computers and other contracts rather than between individuals or organizations.

3.6.3 How Do Smart Contracts Work?

- A smart contract is simply a digital contract that has blockchain security coded into it. It contains permissions and details written in code that need to happen in a precise order for the terms specified in the smart contract to be agreed upon.
- Time restrictions that may result in deadlines in the contract may also be included.
- The concept of smart contracts is quite straightforward. They are carried out using basic logic, such as IF-THEN:
- The amount (of money, in cryptocurrency) will be sent to you if you send object A.
- The A item will be sent to you if you send a specific quantity of digital assets (such as cryptocurrency, like bitcoin or ether).
- The digital materials specified in the contract will be sent to me IF I complete the assignment.

Smart Contract Working

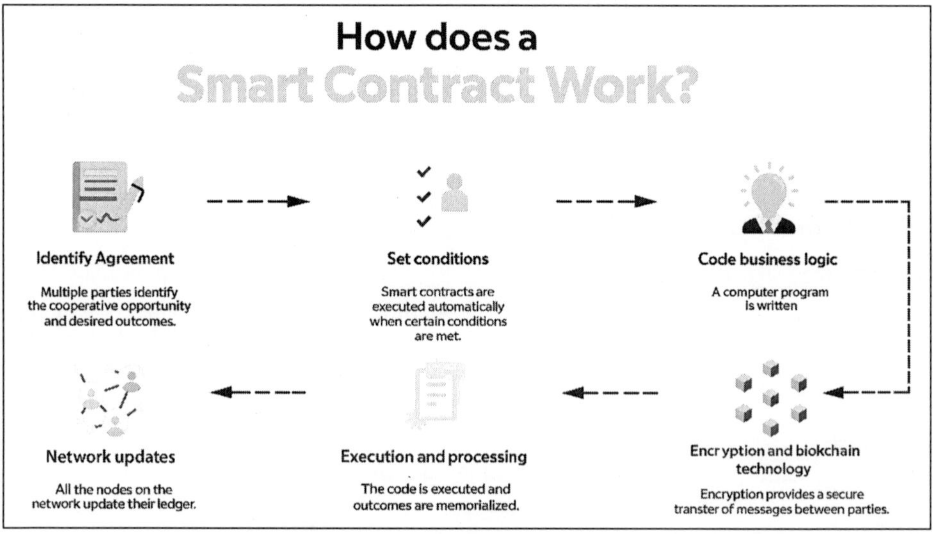

Fig. 3.3: Smart Contract Working

- **Determine Agreement:** Several parties determine the opportunity for cooperation and the intended results. Agreements may include asset swaps, business procedures, etc.
- **Establish conditions:** Parties may launch smart contracts on their own or in response to specific events, such as GPS locations or financial market indexes.
- **Business logic code:** When the conditional parameters are satisfied, a computer program is developed that will run automatically.
- **Blockchain technology and encryption:** Secure authentication and communication exchange between parties pertaining to smart contracts are made possible via encryption.
- **Processing and execution:** In a blockchain iteration, the code is run and the results are recorded for compliance and verification whenever the parties agree on authentication and verification.

- **Network updates:** Every node on the network updates its ledger to reflect the new status following the execution of smart contracts. The record is in append mode only and cannot be changed once it has been posted and validated on the blockchain network.

3.7 FRONT-END CREATION

Front-end development is the construction of the user-visible and user-interactive features of a web site or web application that a user directly perceives and interfaces with. Front-end development consists of everything seen on the user's screen from layouts, graphics, and navigational components down to buttons, images, and animations. It is crucial that front-end be well implemented if a user should have a satisfactory UX and guarantees the site or app is both intuitive and responsively reacting and pleasing to view.

Front-end development in the context of blockchain systems also entails the inclusion of decentralized aspects like blockchain transactions, wallets, and interactions with smart contracts in the user interface. This builds a bridge of continuity between the users and the underlying blockchain systems to facilitate interaction with decentralized apps (dApps) or decentralized finance (DeFi) systems.

3.8 CONNECTING SMART CONTRACT WITH FRONT-END APPLICATION

We will discover how to link a smart contract to the front end in this article. The smart contract itself is kept basic in order to simplify the procedure and concentrate on the integration phase. Once you grasp the fundamentals, you can introduce several sophisticated functions with ease.

In this lesson, we are merely launching a campaign on the local blockchain, which will be displayed on the front end after it has been mined. Since taking the data from the front and putting it back is the most fundamental task, I chose this example. After you master this, you can obviously execute any necessary function on the data and display it on the front page.

Method for Combining your Front-end and Smart Contract

To show how the frontend and smart contracts may work together, we'll be building a straightforward web application.

1. Set up the Next JS application.
2. Next, use the provided command to install the dependencies needed for web3 development.
3. Set up the hardhat environment first.
4. Drafting the smart contract.
5. Composing the script for deployment.
6. Contract deployment.
7. Context folder creation for frontend and smart contract integration.
8. Constructing our app's front end.
9. Utilizing the Web Context service to wrap the layout.
10. Launching the application.

3.8.1 Connecting Smart Contract with Front-End Application Implementation

Step 1: Initialize Next App

Use the command to create a Next JS app and proceed with Javascript:

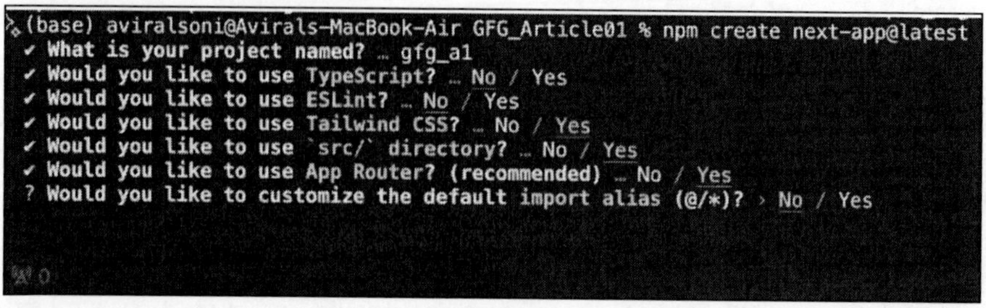

Fig. 3.4

Step 2: Install Dependencies

Run this command to install the required and compatible dependencies:

```
npm install @headlessui/react@^1.7.19 @heroicons/react@^2.1.3
@next/font@^13.2.4 @nomicfoundation/hardhat-toolbox@^2.0.2
autoprefixer@^10.4.19 bufferutil@^4.0.8 ethers@^5.7.2 hardhat@^2.22.3
next@^13.2.4 react@^18.2.0 react-dom@^18.2.0 utf-8-validate@^5.0.10
web3modal@^1.9.12 postcss@^8.4.38 tailwindcss@^3.4.3 --save
```

Managing dependencies can be challenging, especially in the rapidly evolving landscape of web3 development. Conflicting versions can lead to frustration and annoyance among developers. To ensure compatibility and avoid conflicts, use the above command to install dependencies that work seamlessly together.

Step 3: Initialize the Hard Hat Environment

Initialise the hardhat environment by running

npx hardhat init

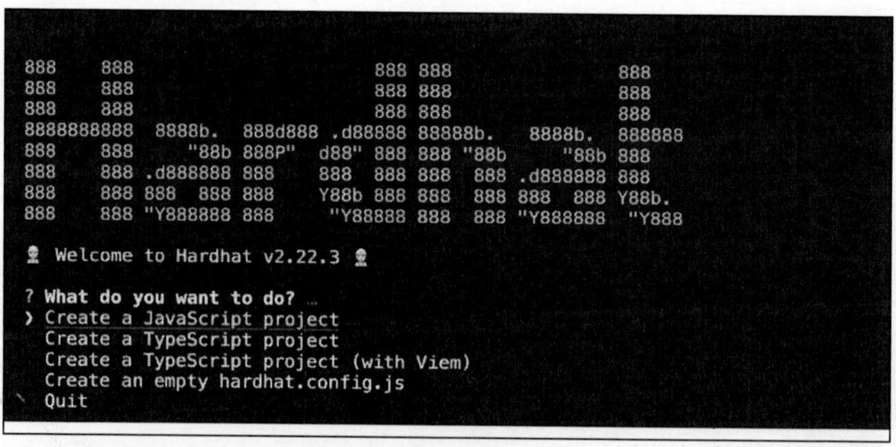

Fig. 3.5: *Initialize HardHat Environment*

Step 4: Writing Smart Contract

After initializing the hardhat env you will notice a 'Contracts' folder has been created. Create a file with the name of your smart contract. Here we are using CrowdFunding.sol.

```
CrowdFunding.sol:
// SPDX-License-Identifier: MIT
pragma solidity ^0.8.0;
contract CrowdFunding {
address public owner;
uint public totalFunds;
uint public target;
bool public campaignEnded;

struct Campaign {
address creator;
string title;
string description;
uint amount;
uint deadline;
uint amountCollected;
bool active;
}
mapping(address => uint) public contributors;
mapping(uint => Campaign) public campaigns;
uint public campaignCounter;
event FundsContributed(address indexed contributor, uint amount);
event CampaignCreated(
address indexed creator,
string title,
uint amount,
uint deadline
);
event CampaignEnded(uint totalFunds, bool succeeded);
constructor(uint _target) {
owner = msg.sender;
target = _target;
campaignEnded = false;
}
modifier onlyOwner() {
require(msg.sender == owner, "Only the owner can call this function");
_;
}
modifier campaignNotEnded() {
require(!campaignEnded, «Campaign has already ended»);
_;
}
```

```
function createCampaign(
string memory _title,
string memory _description,
uint _amount,
uint _deadline
) public campaignNotEnded {
require(_amount > 0, «Contribution amount must be greater than 0»);
require(_deadline > block.timestamp, “Deadline must be in the future”);
campaigns[campaignCounter] = Campaign({
creator: msg.sender,
title: _title,
description: _description,
amount: _amount,
deadline: _deadline,
amountCollected: 0,
active: true
});
campaignCounter++;
emit CampaignCreated(msg.sender, _title, _amount, _deadline);
}
function contribute(uint _campaignId) public payable campaignNotEnded {
require(campaigns[_campaignId].active, «Campaign is not active»);
require(msg.value > 0, “Contribution amount must be greater than 0”);
require(
block.timestamp < campaigns[_campaignId].deadline,
«Campaign deadline has passed»
);
contributors[msg.sender] += msg.value;
campaigns[_campaignId].amountCollected += msg.value;
totalFunds += msg.value;
emit FundsContributed(msg.sender, msg.value);
checkGoalReached(_campaignId);
}
function checkGoalReached(uint _campaignId) private {
if (
campaigns[_campaignId].amountCollected >=
campaigns[_campaignId].amount
) {
campaigns[_campaignId].active = false;
campaignEnded = true;
emit CampaignEnded(totalFunds, true);
}
}
function withdrawFunds() public onlyOwner {
require(campaignEnded, «Campaign has not ended yet»);
```

```
require(address(this).balance >= totalFunds, «Insufficient funds»);
payable(owner).transfer(totalFunds);
}
function getBalance() public view returns (uint) {
return address(this).balance;
}
function getCampaigns() public view returns (Campaign[] memory) {
Campaign[] memory allCampaigns = new Campaign[](campaignCounter);
for (uint i = 0; i < campaignCounter; i++) {
allCampaigns[i] = campaigns[i];
}
return allCampaigns;
}
}
```

Step 5: Writing Deployment Script for the Contract

Create a folder Scripts and create a file named deploy.js. In this file the code for deploying the contract will be written.

```
const { ethers } = require("hardhat");
async function main() {
const CrowdFunding = await ethers.getContractFactory("CrowdFunding");
const crowdFunding = await CrowdFunding.deploy(1000); // Pass the target
amount here (e.g., 1000 wei)
await crowdFunding.deployed();
console.log(«CrowdFunding deployed to:», crowdFunding.address);
}
main()
.then(() => process.exit(0))
.catch((error) => {
console.error(error);
process.exit(1);
});
```

Note: The name of the Contract is passed in the getContractFactory function.

Step 6: Deploying the contract

1. Deploy the smart contract using the command: *npx hardhat node*

   This initialises a local blockchain and gives about 20 addresses with 1000 ETH for testing.

2. You can import any of these accounts in your Metamask wallet by choosing to import the account and then entering the private key.

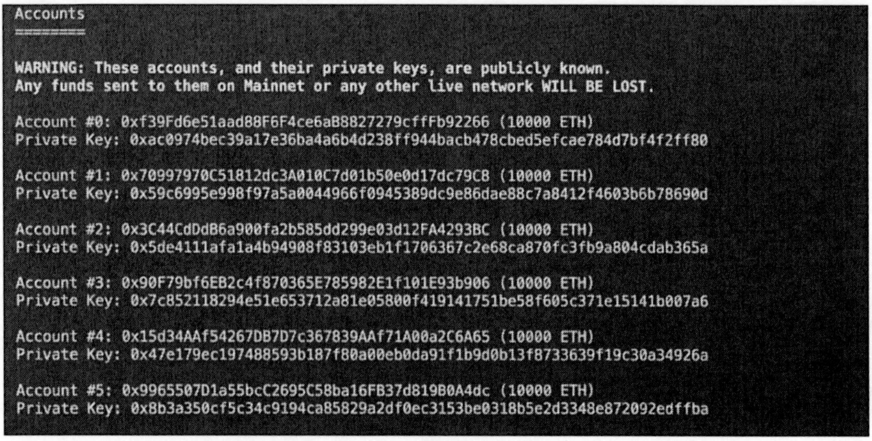

Fig. 3.6: *The accounts after running npx hardhat node*

3. Open another terminal and run the command: *npx hardhat run --network localhost scripts/deploy.js*

   This command will deploy your contract and create a folder called **artifacts.**

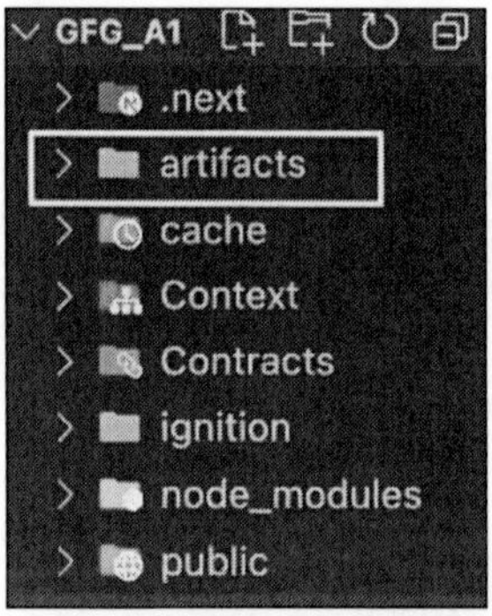

Fig. 3.7: *Artifacts Folder*

4. It will also print the address on which our contract is deployed at.

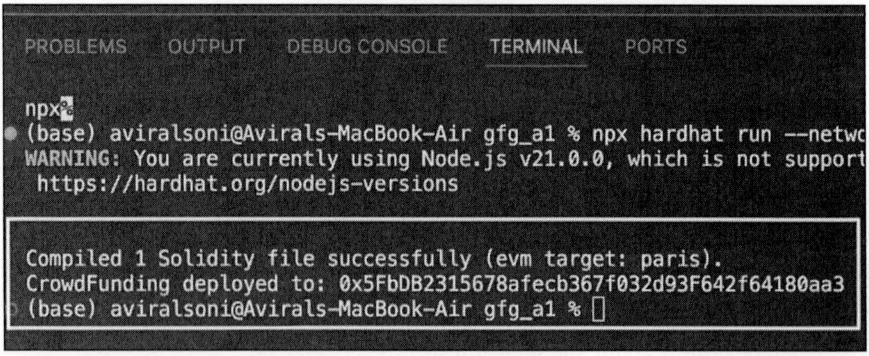

Fig. 3.8: *Contract Address*

Copy this address for now.

Step 7: Create Context Folder

To connect a smart contract with the frontend, we always need a file separate from the frontend file and the smart contract. This file acts like a bridge between the two.

1. Create a folder **Context**, and inside it create a file called **CrowdFunding.js** and **Constants.js**. Constants.js will contains the attributes of the deployed contract, that will be used in the CrowdFunding.js file.

Constants.js (in Context folder):

```
import crowdFunding from './CrowdFunding.json';
export const CROWDFUNDING_ADDRESS
= '0x5FbDB2315678afecb367f032d93F642f64180aa3'; // Update this address
export const CROWDFUNDING_ABI = crowdFunding.abi;
```

Paste the copied address in the field of CROWDFUNDING_ADDRESS.

2. Now have a look at the artifacts folder that had been created after the deployment of the contract. You should see a contracts folder inside it and in the contracts folder, there will be a file called CrowdFunding.json. Move this file from this folder to Context folder (simply by dragging).

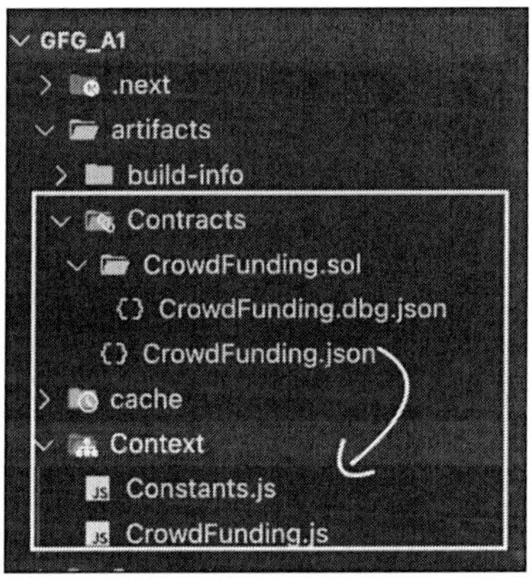

Fig. 3.9: *CrowdFunding.json file has to be moved from artifacts/Contracts to Context folder*

This file will be used to get the **ABI** of the contract from the json file.

3. Write the code for another file inside Context i.e. Crowdfunding.js. This is the file that connects the smart contract with the frontend.

```
Crowdfunding.js:
'use client'
import React, { useState, useEffect } from "react";
import Web3Modal from "web3modal";
import { ethers } from "ethers";
// INTERNAL IMPORTS
import { CROWDFUNDING_ABI, CROWDFUNDING_ADDRESS } from "./Constants";
// FETCHING SMART CONTRACT
```

```
const fetchContract = (signerOrProvider) =>
new      ethers.Contract(CROWDFUNDING_ADDRESS,       CROWDFUNDING_ABI,
signerOrProvider);
export const CrowdFundingContext = React.createContext();
export const CrowdFundingProvider = ({ children }) => {
const titleData = "Crowd Funding";
const [currentAccount, setCurrentAccount] = useState("");
const [error, setError] = useState(null);
const createCampaign = async (campaign) => {
const { title, description, amount, deadline } = campaign;
const web3Modal = new Web3Modal();
const connection = await web3Modal.connect();
const provider = new ethers.providers.Web3Provider(connection);
const signer = provider.getSigner();
const contract = fetchContract(signer);
try {
const transaction = await contract.createCampaign(
title,
description,
ethers.utils.parseUnits(amount, 18),
new Date(deadline).getTime()
);
await transaction.wait();
console.log(«Transaction Mined», transaction);
} catch (error) {
console.log(«Error», error);
}
};
const getCampaigns = async () => {
const provider = new ethers.providers.JsonRpcProvider();
const contract = fetchContract(provider);
const campaigns = await contract.getCampaigns();
const parsedCampaigns = campaigns.map((campaign, i) => ({
owner: campaign.owner,
title: campaign.title,
description: campaign.description,
target:    ethers.utils.formatEther(campaign.amount.toString()),    //
Corrected line
deadline: campaign.deadline.toNumber(),
amountCollected: ethers.utils.formatEther(
campaign.amountCollected.toString()
),
pId: i,
}));
return parsedCampaigns;
};
```

```
const ifWalletConnected = async () => {
try {
if (!window.ethereum) {
setError(«Install Metamask»);
return false;
}
const accounts = await window.ethereum.request({
method: «eth_accounts»,
});
if (accounts.length) {
setCurrentAccount(accounts[0]);
return true;
} else {
console.log(«No account found»);
}
} catch (error) {
console.log(«Something wrong while connecting to the wallet «, error);
return false;
}
};
useEffect(() => {
ifWalletConnected();
}, []);
const connectWallet = async () => {
try {
if (!window.ethereum) {
setError(«Install Metamask»);
return;
}
const accounts = await window.ethereum.request({
method: «eth_requestAccounts»,
});
setCurrentAccount(accounts[0]);
} catch (error) {
console.log(«Something wrong while connecting to the wallet», error);
}
};
return (
<CrowdFundingContext.Provider
value={{
titleData,
currentAccount,
connectWallet,
createCampaign,
getCampaigns,
```

```
error,
}}
>
{children}
</CrowdFundingContext.Provider>
);
};
```

Explanation

1. **fetchContract(signerOrProvider):** Returns an instance of the CrowdFunding smart contract.
2. **createCampaign(campaign):** Creates a new campaign on the blockchain.
3. **getCampaigns():** Retrieves all existing campaigns from the blockchain.
4. **ifWalletConnected():** Checks if the user's wallet is connected.
5. **connectWallet():** Connects the user's wallet to the application.

Step 8: Create Frontend for our Smart Contract

We will be writing some frontend in the page.js file in the src/app folder. This file will contain a button to connect wallet to Metamask wallet. After the connection is made, address of the connected account will be shown instead of the button. It has a form to fill the details of the campaign. After the Campaign has been made, it will be displayed on the page.

```
page.js (inside src/app folder):
'use client'
import Image from "next/image";
import React, { useState, useContext, useEffect } from 'react'
import { CrowdFundingContext } from '../../Context/CrowdFunding'
export default function Home() {
const { createCampaign, error, getCampaigns, currentAccount, connectWallet
} = useContext(CrowdFundingContext)
const [title, setTitle] = useState('')
const [description, setDescription] = useState('')
const [amount, setAmount] = useState('')
const [deadline, setDeadline] = useState('')
const [errorMessage, setErrorMessage] = useState('')
const [campaigns, setCampaigns] = useState([])
const fetchCampaigns = async () => {
try {
const data = await getCampaigns()
setCampaigns(data)
} catch (error) {
console.error('Error while fetching campaigns:', error)
setErrorMessage('Error while fetching campaigns')
}
}
```

```
useEffect(() => {
fetchCampaigns()
}, [])
const handleSubmit = async (e) => {
e.preventDefault()
const campaign = {
title,
description,
amount,
deadline
}
try {
await createCampaign(campaign)
setErrorMessage('')
setTitle('')
setDescription('')
setAmount('')
setDeadline('')
fetchCampaigns()
} catch (error) {
console.error('Error while creating campaign:', error)
setErrorMessage(error.message || 'Error while creating campaign')
}
}
return (
<div style={{ maxWidth: '800px', margin: '0 auto', padding: '20px' }}>
<h1 style={{ fontSize: '24px', fontWeight: 'bold', marginBottom: '10px'
}}>GFG on WEB3</h1>
{!currentAccount ? (
<button
style={{ backgroundColor: '#007bff', color: 'white', border: 'none',
padding: '10px 20px', fontSize: '16px', cursor: 'pointer', marginBottom:
'20px' }}
onClick={connectWallet}
>
Connect Wallet
</button>
) : (
<div style={{ marginBottom: '20px' }}>
<p style={[ marginTop: '10px' }}>Connected Wallet: {currentAccount}</p>
</div>
)}
<h2 style={{ fontSize: '20px', fontWeight: 'bold', marginTop: '20px'
}}>Create Campaign</h2>
<form onSubmit={handleSubmit} style={{ marginTop: '20px' }}>
<div style={{ marginBottom: '10px' }}>
```

```
<label style={{ display: 'block', fontSize: '16px', marginBottom: '5px'
}}>Title:</label>
<input
style={{ width: '100%', padding: '10px' }}
type='text'
value={title}
onChange={e => setTitle(e.target.value)}
/>
</div>
<div style={{ marginBottom: '10px' }}>
<label style={{ display: 'block', fontSize: '16px', marginBottom: '5px'
}}>Description:</label>
<textarea
style={{ width: '100%', padding: '10px' }}
value={description}
onChange={e => setDescription(e.target.value)}
/>
</div>
<div style={{ marginBottom: '10px' }}>
<label style={{ display: 'block', fontSize: '16px', marginBottom: '5px'
}}>Amount:</label>
<input
style={{ width: '100%', padding: '10px' }}
type='number'
value={amount}
onChange={e => setAmount(e.target.value)}
/>
</div>
<div style={{ marginBottom: '10px' }}>
<label style={{ display: 'block', fontSize: '16px', marginBottom: '5px'
}}>Deadline:</label>
<input
style={{ width: '100%', padding: '10px' }}
type='date'
value={deadline}
onChange={e => setDeadline(e.target.value)}
/>
</div>
<button
type='submit'
style={{ backgroundColor: '#007bff', color: 'white', border: 'none',
padding: '10px 20px', fontSize: '16px', cursor: 'pointer', marginTop:
'10px' }}
>
Create Campaign
</button>
```

```
{errorMessage && <p style={{ color: 'red', marginTop: '10px'
}}>{errorMessage}</p>}
</form>
<h2 style={{ fontSize: '20px', fontWeight: 'bold', marginTop: '20px'
}}>Campaigns</h2>
<div>
{campaigns.map((campaign, index) => (
<div key={index} style={{ border: '1px solid #ccc', borderRadius: '5px',
padding: '10px', marginTop: '20px' }}>
<h3 style={{ fontSize: '18px', fontWeight: 'bold' }}>{campaign.title}</
h3>
<p>Description: {campaign.description}</p>
<p>Target Amount: {campaign.target}</p>
<p>Deadline: {new Date(campaign.deadline).toLocaleDateString()}</p>
</div>
))}
</div>
</div>
);
}
```

Step 9: Wrap the Layout Inside the Web3 Provider

Wrap the children inside the layout.js(in src) with CrowdFundingProvider that we made in CrowdFunding.js(Context).

```
src/layout.js:
import { Inter } from "next/font/google";
import "./globals.css";
import {CrowdFundingProvider} from '../../Context/CrowdFunding'
import Form from "../../Components/Form";
const inter = Inter({ subsets: ["latin"] });
export const metadata = {
title: "GFG App",
description: "Integrating front-end with smart contracts",
};
export default function RootLayout({ children }) {
return (
<>
 <html lang="en">
<body className={inter.className}>
<CrowdFundingProvider>
<div>
</div>
{children}
</CrowdFundingProvider>
 </body>
```

```
</html>
</>
);
}
```

Step 10: Execute the Application

1. Run the command:

   npm run dev

   If you get an error related to - The `app` directory is experimental, then modify the next.config.mjs in the following manner:

```
/** @type {import('next').NextConfig} */
const nextConfig = {
experimental: {
appDir: true,
},
};
export default nextConfig;
```

2. After Running npm run dev, you should be able to see this page:

Fig. 3.10: Home Page for our App

3. On clicking the **Connect Wallet** button a Metamask window will popup and after you select the account you want to connect with the contract address will be visible on the site in place of the button.

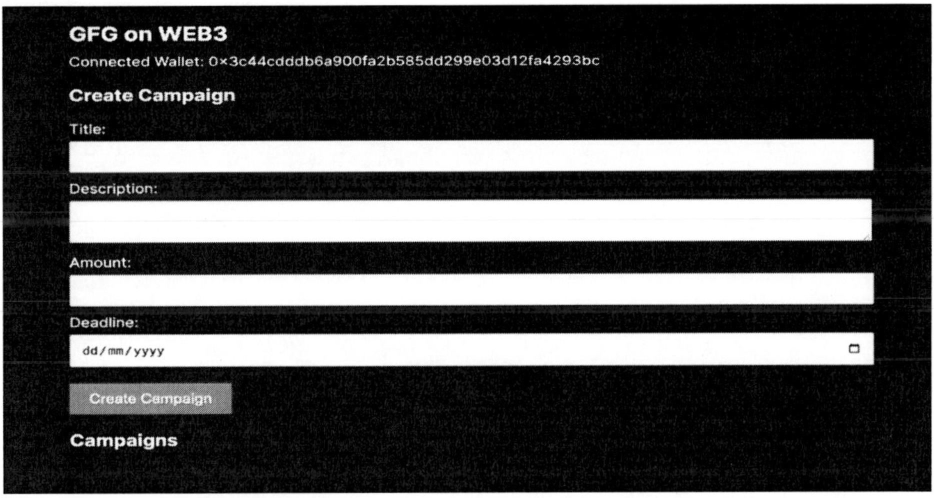

Fig. 3.11: Account Connected and Wallet Address Displayed

4. Fill in the form fields.

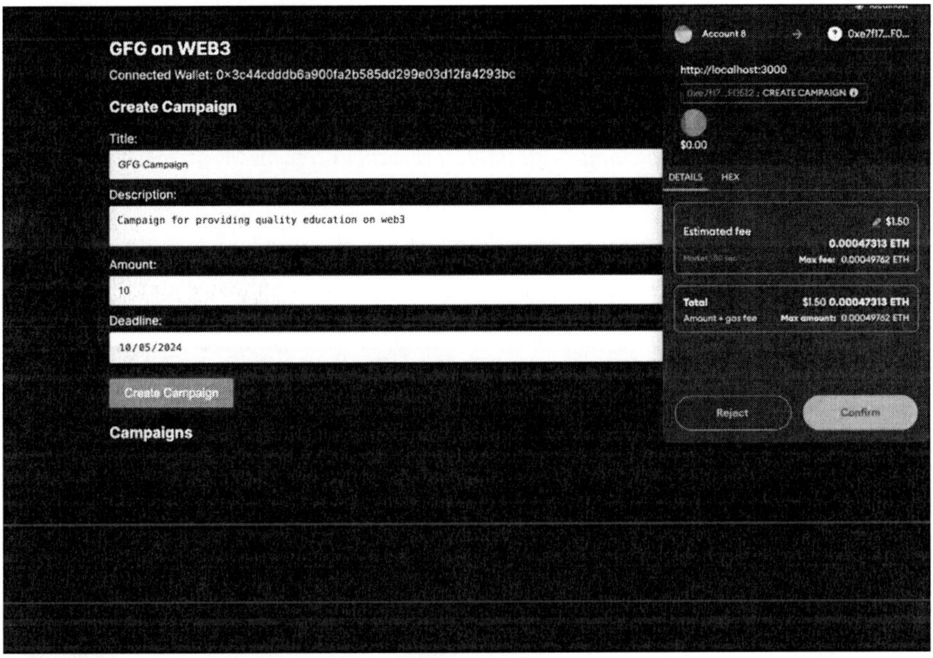

Fig. 3.12: Create Campaign

5. After you click on the **Create Campaign** button a Metamask notification should pop up, asking for confirmation for the payment. This payment is the gas fee. Click on confirm and a campaign will be added to the list.

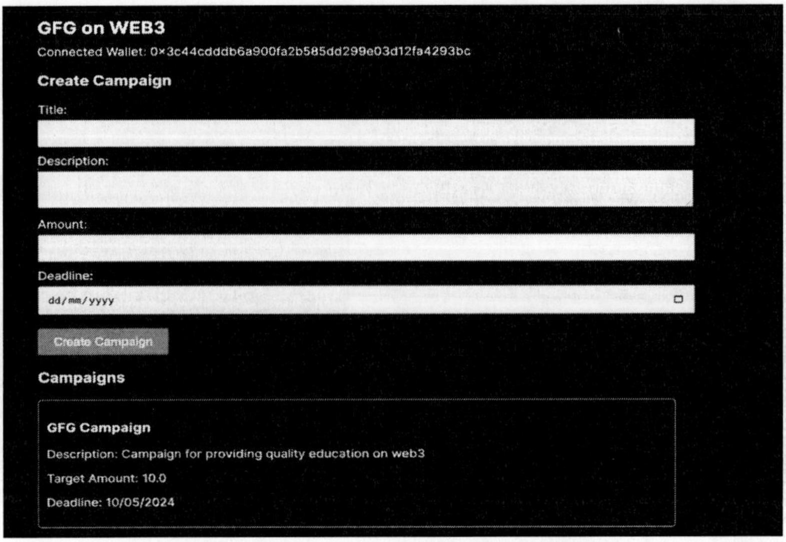

Fig. 3.13: *Campaign is created and displayed!*

Note:

1. *Every time you redeploy your contract you need to change the contract address in the constants.js file. Also you have to delete the Contract.json file from the Context and paste the new one from the artifacts.*
2. *You can add the accounts with 1000 ETH each, by copying the private keys that come on the terminal after running npx hardhat node.*

Step 11: Importing Accounts in Metamask Wallet

1. Click on the **Metamask extension**. Login and click on the Account that comes on the top of pop up.

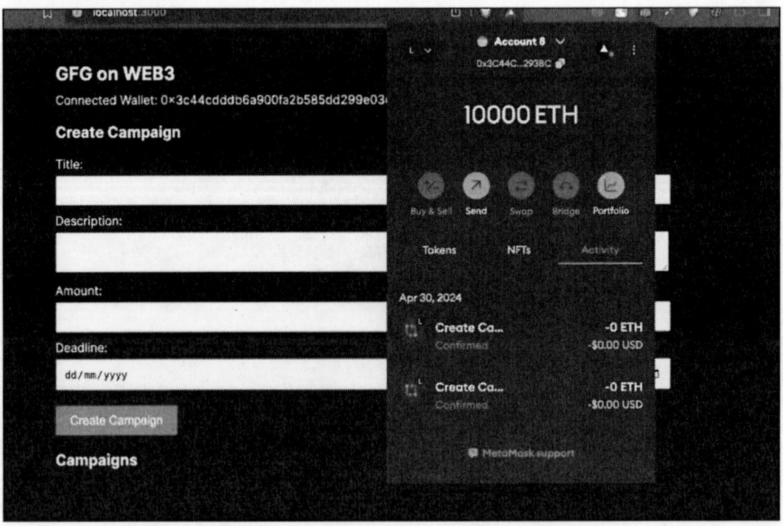

Fig. 3.14: *Click on the Account Name (Account8)*

2. Click on **Add account or hardware wallet.**

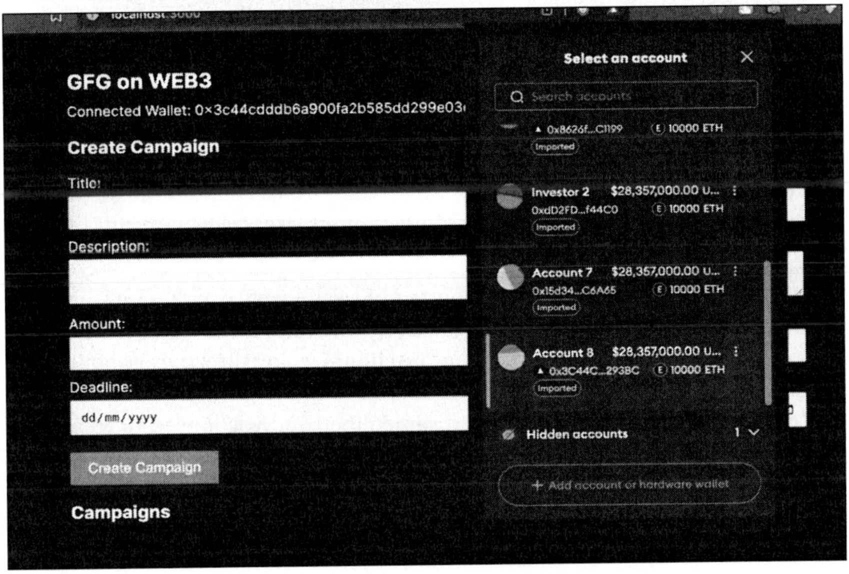

Fig. 3.15: Click on Add Account or hardware wallet.

3. Click on **Import account.**

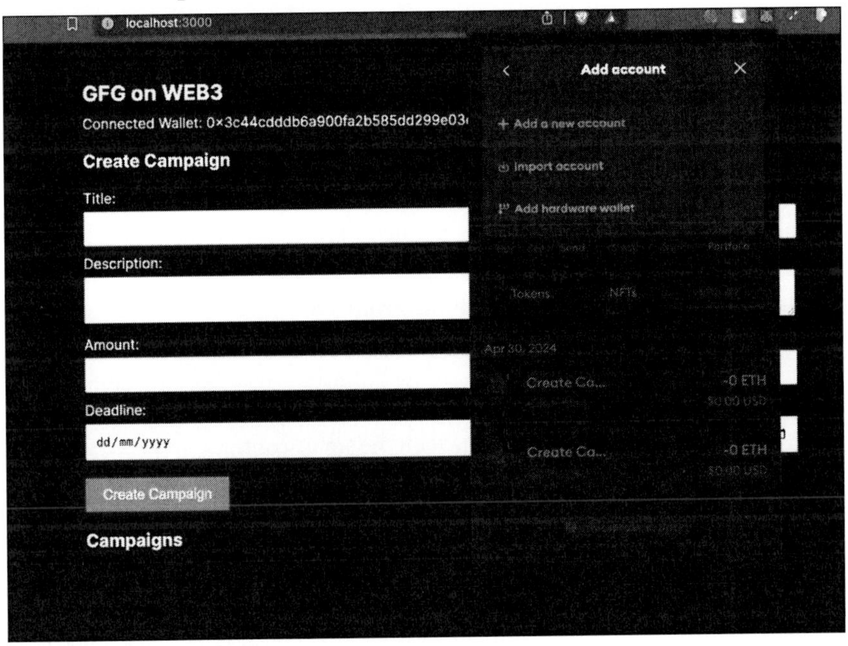

Fig. 3.16: Choose import account.

4. Paste the private key from the terminal as the output of run the command: *npx hardhat node.*

3.9 DEPLOYING DAPP

From creating smart contracts to installing the front end and communicating with the blockchain, implementing a Decentralized Application (DApp) usually entails a number of processes. This is a general outline of the procedure:

1. **Development of Smart Contracts:** Create the smart contracts: Solidity is usually used to write smart contracts (for Ethereum or comparable blockchains). In these contracts, you specify the reasoning behind your application.Examine smart contracts: Make that the contracts function as expected by testing them with frameworks such as Truffle, Hardhat, or Synthesis.
2. **Add Blockchain:** Based Smart Contracts:Select a Network: Before launching on the mainnet, you can deploy to a testnet (such as Rinkeby, Ropsten, or Sepolia for Ethereum).Put the Contracts into Action: Deploy the smart contracts on the blockchain using programs like Hardhat, Truffle, or Remix. To pay for gas fees (even on testnets), you might need some Ether, and you'll need to communicate with the blockchain using wallets like MetaMask.
3. **Front-end programming:** Build the front end: For the front end, use libraries such as React, Angular, or Vue.js. You will use a wallet (such as MetaMask) to communicate with your smart contract by integrating Web3.js or Ethers.js.
   - **Connect the smart contract to the front end:** To read from and write to the blockchain, your DApp front-end will communicate with the deployed smart contract using Web3.js or Ethers.js.
4. **Install Front:** End Software on a Static Web Hosting Platform: When the front-end is complete, it can be hosted on websites such as
   - **InterPlanetary File System, or IPFS:** This guarantees your front-end is decentralized. You can pin your files to IPFS by using services like Pinata or Infura.
   - **Conventional Web Hosting Services:** For a more conventional setup, you can also use cloud providers such as AWS, Netlify, or Vercel.
5. **Connecting Smart Contract with the Front-End**
   - **MetaMask Integration:** To enable users to engage with your DApp and sign transactions, utilize MetaMask or another wallet that is compatible with Ethereum. The Web3 provider is injected into the browser by MetaMask, allowing you to communicate with the smart contract.
6. **Testing the DApp Test on Testnets:** It is essential to test your DApp on a test network to ensure that everything works as it should before deploying to the mainnet.
   - **Updates and Bug Fixes:** Any issues should be resolved and re-released.
7. **Monitor and Maintain Monitoring:** Keep an eye on the functionality and activity of your smart contract by using services like Forta or Tenderly.
   - **Gas Optimization:** If you're using Ethereum for deployment, make sure your smart contract is set up to pay less for gas.

Example Tools for DApp Deployment

- **Truffle/Hardhat**: For smart contract development, deployment, and testing.
- **React/Vue/Angular**: For front-end development.
- **Ethers.js/Web3.js**: For interacting with smart contracts from the front-end.
- **MetaMask**: As a browser wallet to interact with your DApp.
- **IPFS/Pinata/Infura**: For decentralized file hosting.
- **Netlify/Vercel**: For traditional hosting.

3.10 VALIDATION AND TESTING OF DAPP

1. **Smart Contract Testing Unit Testing**: Verify the accuracy of smart contract operations using frameworks like as Hardhat or Truffle.

   Integration testing involves emulating actual transactions by testing contract interactions on testnets such as Rinkeby or Sepolia.

   Security audits: To find vulnerabilities, run automated tools (like MythX and Slither) and do manual checks.
2. **Front-End Testing Unit Testing**: To test distinct functionality and components, use the Jest or React Testing Libraries.

   Integration Testing: Use Web3.js or Ethers.js to test the front-end's communication with deployed contracts.

   End-to-End Testing: To test the entire DApp experience (wallet interactions, transactions), tools such as Cypress mimic user journeys.
3. **Evaluation of Performance:** Load Testing: Simulate heavy user traffic with tools like Artillery.

   Gas Optimization: Keep an eye on gas prices and optimize them for smart contract operations.
4. **User Acceptance Testing (UAT):** To find errors, usability problems, and opportunities for improvement, get input from a small user group.
5. **Implementation of Testnets:** Before going live, deploy your DApp on a testnet to test it in real-world scenarios using fictitious ether.
6. **Monitoring After Deployment:** For continuous testing and real-time monitoring to guarantee continued functionality, use services like Forta or Tenderly.

EXERCISE

Building a Crowdfunding Platform

- **Situation**: You are developing a crowdfunding platform that allows project creators to raise money from backers and releases money when funding milestones are achieved.
- **Tasks**:
  - **Project Creation:** creators set project objectives, funding targets, and deadlines.

    - **Funding Process:** Facilitate backers to safely contribute money.
    - Provide a system to refund backers when funding targets are not achieved within the deadline.
- **Milestone Management:**
    - Establish funding milestones that release funds to the creator of the project upon confirmation.Make transparency available to supporters about fund usage.

SUMMARY

Smart contracts are computer programs that are coded on a blockchain and automatically enforce and execute the terms of an agreement when specific conditions are satisfied. For instance, they can be compared to vending machines: after inserting the right amount of money and choosing an item, the machine delivers the selected product without any human intervention. These electronic contracts eliminate the need for intermediaries, lower the cost of transaction, and improve the efficiency and security of contractual arrangements in a wide range of industries. ’

Performance Related Issues

4 UNIT

4.1 TRANSACTION SPEED

Transaction speed is an essential consideration when measuring the performance of any blockchain network. It describes the duration it takes to process, confirm, and validate a transaction within the blockchain. In order for blockchain systems to be practical and scalable enough for daily applications, transaction speed needs to be optimized to provide speedy and efficient interactions.

4.2 TRANSACTION FEES

Transaction fees can vary greatly depending on network activity; high fees during peak times make certain blockchains less appealing for microtransactions.

4.3 NETWORK SIZE

A larger network can offer better security and decentralization but may also increase latency and resource requirements for nodes.

4.4 TRANSACTION SPEED

Some blockchains, like Bitcoin, have slower transaction speeds due to network congestion and consensus mechanisms (e.g., Proof of Work). This can affect usability for real-time transactions.

4.5 COMPLEXITY

The need for specialized knowledge to develop and implement blockchain technology can be a barrier to adoption for developers and businesses.

4.6 INTEROPERABILITY ISSUES

Since many blockchains function independently, it can be challenging to move assets and data between networks without the assistance of third parties.

4.7 LACK OF STANDARDIZATION

Distinct protocols, smart contract languages, and governance models lead to fragmentation, which makes it more difficult for companies to integrate blockchain solutions across various platforms.

4.7.1 Lack of Supportive Regulations Related to Blockchain Applications

One of the main obstacles to the implementation of blockchain technology is regulatory ambiguity. Blockchain-based applications are still being categorized and regulated by governments and regulatory agencies around the world. Among the main concerns are:

1. **Legal Cryptocurrency Classification:** Inconsistent regulations result from the debate in many nations over whether cryptocurrencies should be regarded as securities, commodities, or currencies.
2. KYC/AML requirements and compliance the decentralized structure of blockchain frequently conflicts with regulatory frameworks such as Know Your Customer (KYC) and Anti-Money Laundering (AML) rules, making compliance challenging.
3. Problems with taxes Crypto transactions are treated very differently by different governments; some treat them as property, while others see them as income. For both individuals and businesses, this lack of consistency makes financial reporting more difficult.
4. **Legality of Smart Contracts:** Because self-executing code is not always taken into account by traditional contract law, there are questions over whether smart contracts are legally enforceable in many places.
5. Rules Across Boundaries Since blockchain is a worldwide technology, companies wishing to conduct business abroad face obstacles due to disparities in country rules.
6. **Security and Consumer Protection:** Stricter (or ambiguous) regulations that could hinder innovation are the result of numerous governments' worries about fraud, scams, and the security of blockchain projects.

4.8 PERFORMANCE IMPROVEMENTS

1. State Channels Off-Chain

Participants can carry out several off-chain transactions using state channels, only sending the final state to the blockchain.

Ethereum's Raiden Network and Bitcoin's Lightning Network are two examples.

Advantages

1. Almost instantaneous transfers.
2. Lower transaction costs.
3. Reduced main chain congestion.

2. Sidechains

Assets and data can be moved across sidechains, which are separate blockchains that are joined to the main chain by a two-way peg.

For instance, Polygon, Ethereum's sidechain, has the advantage of offloading transactions from the main chain.

Lessens congestion and improves scalability. Enables testing of novel features without impacting the primary network.

4.9 PARA CHAINS, OR PARALLEL CHAINS

A collection of blockchains linked to a central relay chain that operate concurrently.

For instance, Polka dot's Parchin Model Offers the following advantages:

1. Every Para chain has a distinct use case.
2. Increases the throughput of transactions.
3. Improves the interoperability of various chains.

4.10 CONCURRENT SMART CONTRACT TRANSACTIONS

Instead of executing smart contracts sequentially, blockchain networks are optimizing execution to process multiple transactions simultaneously.

Example: Aptos and Sui leverage parallel execution methods for faster throughput.

Benefits

1. Reduces bottlenecks in transaction processing.
2. Improves the overall effectiveness of the network.

4.11 SHARDING TECHNIQUE AND ITS BENEFITS

By using sharding, the blockchain is split up into separate sections, or shards, that may individually handle transactions on their own.

For instance, the upcoming sharding implementation in Ethereum 2.0.

Benefits

1. Processes operations in parallel, increasing transaction throughput.
2. Lessens the strain on specific nodes.
3. Makes large-scale blockchain applications more scalable.

4.12 ATOMIC SWAPS BETWEEN SMART CONTRACTS

Atomic swaps allow for peer-to-peer, trustless transactions between various cryptocurrencies and smart contracts without the need for middlemen.

Example: Hashed Timelock Contracts (HTLCs) for Bitcoin-Ethereum Atomic Swaps.

Advantages

1. Eliminates the need for centralized exchanges.
2. Lowers the risk of counterparties.
3. Improves blockchain networks' compatibility with one another.

EXERCISE

Scenario 1: Gas Optimization

A decentralized application (DApp) has high transaction fees because of inefficient smart contract code, and users are unhappy.

- **Question**: What would you do to optimize the gas consumption of the smart contract and minimize transaction costs?

SUMMARY

Smart contracts, though bringing the benefits of automation and efficiency, come with a number of performance-related issues that need to be weighed with caution. Gas optimization, security loopholes, network overload, code maintainability, and dealing with the untoward become critical factors influencing their performance. Overcoming these issues calls for in-depth knowledge of developing smart contracts, such as optimization techniques, security standards, performance tuning, maintainability, and sound testing practices. Identifying and addressing potential issues in advance is important to ensure reliable, secure, and effective smart contracts that increase user confidence and the general success of decentralized applications.

Challenges in Blockchain

5

UNIT

5.1 OPPORTUNITIES IN BLOCKCHAIN TECHNOLOGY

Although blockchain technology has the potential to revolutionize a number of industries, there are also many obstacles to overcome. A summary of the main prospects and difficulties is provided below.

1. Increased Transparency and Security

- Data is visible and impenetrable due to blockchain's decentralized structure and cryptographic protection.
- Applications include identity verification, financial transactions, and supply chain tracking.

2. Innovation in Decentralized Finance (DeFi)

- DeFi makes direct financial transactions possible by doing away with middlemen like banks.
- Applications include decentralized exchanges (Uniswap, SushiSwap), and lending systems (Aave, Compound).

3. Automation using Smart Contracts

- Contracts that execute themselves simplify corporate procedures and do away with reliance on third parties.
- Applications include insurance claims, real estate, and contracts.

4. International Remittances and Payments

- overseas transactions that are quicker and less expensive than those conducted through regular financial channels.
- Applications include stable coins (USDT, USDC), Stellar (XLM), and Ripple (XRP).

5. Asset Tokenization

- It is possible to tokenize and safely exchange both digital and physical assets, such as equities, real estate, and artwork.
- Applications include fractional real estate ownership and NFTs.

6. Better Management of the Supply Chain

- Blockchain guarantees product validity and end-to-end visibility.
- Applications include IBM Food Trust and Walmart (food safety tracking).

7. Authentication and Identity Management

- Digital identities based on blockchain increase security and lower fraud.
- Applications include voting systems, self-sovereign identities, and KYC (Know Your Customer).

8.Compatibility In between Blockchains

- Data sharing and communication between blockchains are made possible by solutions like Chain-link, Cosmos, and Polka dot.

5.2 APPLICATION OF BLOCK CHAIN

5.2.1 Industry 4.0

Industry 4.0, also known as the Fourth Industrial Revolution, incorporates sophisticated technologies such as IoT, AI, Big Data, Robotics, and Blockchain to boost automation, efficiency, and decision-making in industries. Blockchain is essential for facilitating safe, open, and decentralized operations in a variety of industries.

Blockchain is essential to Industry 4.0 because it improves automation, security, and transparency in a number of industries. As demonstrated by IBM Food Trust, it guarantees real-time tracking and guards against counterfeiting in supply chain management. Blockchain facilitates machine-to-machine (M2M) transactions and protects data integrity for Industrial IoT (IIoT). Blockchain is being used in smart manufacturing by Siemens and Bosch to automate production and predictive maintenance. Peer-to-peer (P2P) energy trades are made possible by decentralized energy trading systems such as Power Ledger. With businesses like GE Aviation tracking airplane components, digital twin technology benefits from blockchain's secure asset management. Furthermore, by offering tamper-proof ownership records, blockchain safeguards intellectual property. In workforce management, it also validates employee credentials using tools like Blockcerts. In Industry 4.0, the main advantages of blockchain are increased security, increased interoperability, cost savings, increased efficiency, and transparency. Smarter and more autonomous systems will be fueled by blockchain adoption as industries continue their digital revolution.

5.2.2 Machine to Machine communication

Machine-to-Machine (M2M) communication refers to the automatic exchange of data between industrial devices without human intervention. This is a core element of Industry 4.0, enabling smart factories, automated logistics, and AI-driven production processes. However, traditional M2M communication relies on centralized servers, making it vulnerable to cyberattacks, data breaches, and inefficiencies. Blockchain technology enhances M2M communication by offering decentralized security, ensuring that data exchanged between industrial IoT (IIoT) devices remains tamper-proof. Smart contracts further automate industrial transactions, such as real-time payments, resource allocation, and predictive maintenance. Companies like Bosch and Siemens leverage blockchain to secure M2M interactions, ensuring data integrity, operational efficiency, and trust among connected devices.

5.3 DATA MANAGEMENT IN INDUSTRY 4.0

Massive volumes of data are produced by Industry 4.0's robotics, industrial automation systems, and Internet of Things devices. However, issues like data silos, cybersecurity threats, and expensive storage are problems for conventional data management solutions. Blockchain's decentralized storage, unchangeable records, and automated compliance systems revolutionize industrial data management. Blockchain guarantees real-time access to precise and impenetrable data for various industry stakeholders by doing away with middlemen. Supply chain visibility, predictive maintenance, and quality control especially benefit from this. Blockchain is used by businesses such as General Electric (GE) to monitor and verify supply chain data, which lowers inefficiencies and guards against fraud in industrial processes.

5.4 FUTURE PROSPECTS

Considering development in AI, 5G, and edge computing enabling smarter and more autonomous industrial ecosystems, blockchain's future in Industry 4.0 looks bright. Blockchain-integrated digital twins, which use blockchain-secured real-time data to virtually reflect real-world industrial assets, are one of the significant advancements. Additionally, industries will be able to efficiently fractionalize and trade resources thanks to tokenized asset management. Large-scale industrial applications will be able to embrace blockchain due to improved scalability provided by Layer 2 solutions (such as rollups and sidechains). Supply chain logistics, machine performance monitoring, and industrial compliance will all be automated in the upcoming years by AI-driven smart contracts, improving operational efficiency, security, and transparency.

5.5 BLOCKCHAIN IN HEALTH 4.0

In order to build a more integrated, effective, and patient-focused healthcare system, Health 4.0 combines IoT, AI, Big Data, and Blockchain. Blockchain is essential for decentralized clinical trials, data interoperability, patient identity verification, and the security of electronic health records (EHRs). Blockchain guarantees that medical data stays tamper-proof, accessible only by authorized individuals, and safe from cyber attacks, in contrast to traditional healthcare databases that are vulnerable to security breaches. Blockchain also makes it easier to trace drugs transparently, which keeps fake medications out of the supply chain. For example, MediLedger uses blockchain technology to improve the security of the pharmaceutical supply chain, guaranteeing that patients only receive genuine medications.

5.6 BLOCKCHAIN PROPERTIES IN HEALTHCARE

Blockchain is ideally suited for healthcare applications because of a number of important features. Reliance on centralized health data servers is eliminated through decentralization, which lowers the possibility of hacking and system breakdowns. While protecting patient anonymity, transparency guarantees that authorized physicians and hospitals can safely access patient records. Trust in healthcare data is ensured by immutability, which stops unauthorized changes to medical histories. The smooth flow of data between various healthcare providers is made possible by interoperability, which enhances patient care continuity. Blockchain is a potent instrument for guaranteeing efficiency, security, and confidence in contemporary healthcare systems because of these characteristics.

5.7 IMPACT ON HEALTHCARE COSTS

Healthcare expenses have increased steadily year after year, with the American healthcare system alone spending billions of dollars each year on medical care, drugs, administrative expenses, and so on. Much of these expenses are due to inefficiencies, mistakes, and the absence of interoperability among systems. Blockchain can lower healthcare expenses in the following manners:

A. Administrative Efficiency

- **Streamlining administrative processes:** Blockchain's distributed nature and smart contracts can automate numerous administrative processes, curtailing the roles of intermediaries, eliminating paperwork, and diminishing errors. For instance, blockchain can facilitate streamlining claims handling and billing, minimizing administrative overhead and fraud detection cost.
- **Increased billing transparency:** Blockchain can offer transparent, clear, and unalterable records of services provided. This facilitates the ease of tracking patients' healthcare expenses, thus decreasing disputes and delays in billing processes.

B. Fraud Reduction

- **Decreasing fraudulent activity:** Blockchain's tamper-proof ledger makes all transactions and records unalterable, which makes it harder for fraud to take place. This would decrease fraud in medicare claims, insurance fraud, and pharmaceutical billing. Healthcare fraud is estimated to cost the U.S. healthcare system billions of dollars each year.
- **Authentication of credentials:** Blockchain can be applied to authenticate healthcare provider credentials and transparency in the medical supply chain. Making sure that doctors, nurses, and medical staff are up to standard lowers malpractice and liability costs.

C. Supply Chain Optimization

- **Supply chain tracking:** Blockchain has the potential to make the medical supply chain more transparent, ensuring medications and medical devices are authentic and have been stored and shipped appropriately. This eliminates the likelihood of counterfeit items making it into the supply chain, potentially causing costly recalls or harming people's health.
- **Low-cost procurement:** By automating the entire supply chain and providing more cost visibility, blockchain can make medical supply procurement cheaper, which can reduce overall healthcare costs.

5.8 IMPACT ON HEALTHCARE VALUE

Healthcare value is a term that goes beyond mere costs and outcomes; it also encompasses maximizing the overall patient experience and ensuring that resources are utilized efficiently to provide the best possible care. Blockchain can be a key driver of improving healthcare value in the following ways:

1. Value-Based Healthcare

- **Enabling value-based models:** The transition from fee-for-service models to value-based healthcare (which is centered on patient outcomes instead of volume of services) is a top priority in most healthcare systems. Blockchain can aid value-based care by allowing precise and real-time monitoring of patient outcomes, assisting providers in aligning incentives with improved health outcomes instead of the number of services delivered.
- **Care coordination smart contracts:** Blockchain's smart contract feature enables healthcare providers to develop automated contracts that reward providers for patient outcomes and quality of care. For instance, if a set of treatment objectives is achieved for a patient, the smart contract automatically initiates a financial reward, encouraging value-based care.
- Reduction of Duplicate Testing and Unnecessary Treatments.
- **Avoiding duplicate testing:** With blockchain's capability to offer a single, unalterable source of patient information, patients will no longer have to repeat the same tests, cutting the cost of unnecessary diagnostics. This also saves time and hassle for patients.
- **Improved decision-making in treatment:** With a comprehensive and accurate medical history, providers can make better-informed decisions, minimizing the chance of unnecessary or ineffective treatment prescriptions, hence enhancing the value of care provided.

2. Simplified Reimbursement and Incentives

- **Speedier, correct payments:** Blockchain will make the reimbursement process for healthcare providers quicker by offering correct and validated information about services provided.
- Smart contracts make automated reimbursement possible, eliminating the need for administrative work by providing immediate and correct payments and making the system more efficient overall.
- **Incentivizing preventive care:** Blockchain can facilitate new incentive programs that reward patients and healthcare providers for taking preventive care measures, for example, vaccinations, screenings, and wellness checks. This redirection toward preventive care can lead to improved health outcomes, lower long-term healthcare expenses, and more satisfied patients.

5.9 CHALLENGES OF USING BLOCKCHAIN FOR HEALTHCARE DATA

Blockchain use in healthcare is fraught with difficulties, despite its advantages. Because regulations like the GDPR (Europe) and HIPAA (USA) demand stringent patient data protection and privacy procedures, regulatory compliance is a major challenge. Blockchain must adhere to these rules without sacrificing its decentralized structure. Limitations in scalability and storage are also problematic because it might be expensive and ineffective to store extensive medical records on the blockchain. This problem can be lessened with the aid of solutions like off-chain storage (IPFS, AR weave). Since many hospitals continue to use antiquated electronic medical record (EMR) systems, integrating with current healthcare systems presents another difficulty. Adoption by the entire industry and defined protocols are necessary for the shift to blockchain-based solutions.

EXERCISE

Scenario 1: Scalability Issues

A supply chain management system using a blockchain is slow and has higher transaction fees when the number of transacting parties and transactions increases.

- **Question**: What would you do to improve the scalability of the blockchain network in this scenario?

SUMMARY

Blockchain technology, as much as it presents revolutionary potential, is confronted with a number of challenges that limit its mass adoption and efficacy. Some of the main challenges include scalability constraints, regulatory compliance issues, interoperability challenges, security risks, and environmental issues in terms of energy usage. Overcoming these challenges requires concerted efforts from technologists, regulators, and industry players to create scalable, secure, and sustainable blockchain solutions that are compatible with current legal and environmental frameworks.